MORAL REGULATION

Edited by Mark Smith

First published in Great Britain in 2015 by

Policy Press
University of Bristol
1-9 Old Park Hill
Bristol
BS2 8BB
UK
t: +44 (0)117 954 5940
pp-info@bristol.ac.uk
www.policypress.co.uk

North America office:
Policy Press
c/o The University of Chicago Press
1427 East 60th Street
Chicago, IL 60637, USA
t: +1 773 702 7700
f: +1 773-702-9756
sales@press.uchicago.edu
www.press.uchicago.edu

ISBN 978-1-4473-2200-9 Paperback
ISBN 978-1-4473-2201-6 ePub
ISBN 978-1-4473-2202-3 Kindle

British Library Cataloguing in Publication Data
A catalogue record for this book is available from the British Library.

Library of Congress Cataloging-in-Publication Data
A catalog record for this book has been requested.

Cover design by Policy Press
Printed in Great Britain by www.4edge.co.uk

ALSO AVAILABLE IN THIS SERIES

GENDER AND FAMILY edited by Viviene E. Cree

CHILDHOOD AND YOUTH edited by Gary Clapton

THE STATE edited by Viviene E. Cree

The complete volume, *Revisiting Moral Panics*, including
a commentary by Charles Critcher

Contents

Contributors

Michaela Benson is a Senior Lecturer in Sociology at Goldsmiths, University of London. She has written extensively on lifestyle migration and has research interests in migration, social class and the sociology of place and space. Her recent book is *Understanding lifestyle migration: Theoretical approaches to migration and the quest for a better way of life* (2014), edited with Nick Osbaldiston.

Katharine Charsley is a Senior Lecturer in the School for Sociology Politics and International Studies at the University of Bristol. Recent publications include an edited collection *Transnational marriage* (2012) and an ethnographic monograph: *Transnational Pakistani connections: Marrying 'back home'* (2013).

Gary Clapton is a Senior Lecturer in Social Work at the University of Edinburgh. He specialises in adoption and fostering, child welfare and protection and fathers. His work includes *Social work with fathers: Positive practice* (2013) and a number of papers directed to changing current policies and practices in Scotland.

Colin Clark is Professor of Sociology and Social Policy at the University of the West of Scotland. His teaching and research interests are mainly located within the broad field of ethnic and racial studies, including issues of mobility, identity, citizenship and language. A recent paper is 'Glasgow's Ellis Island? The integration and stigmatisation of Govanhill's Roma population' (2014), *People, Place and Policy*, vol 8, no 1, pp 34–50.

Viviene E. Cree is Professor of Social Work Studies at the University of Edinburgh. She is a qualified youth and community and social worker. She has carried out extensive research into social work history, the profession and children's services and has published widely. A recent book is *Becoming a social worker: Global narratives* (2013).

Frank Furedi is a sociologist, commentator and author. He is currently working on the sociological history of the relation between morality and the performance of fear. He published *Moral crusades in an age of mistrust: The Jimmy Savile Scandal* in 2013.

David Grumett is Chancellor's Fellow in Christian Ethics and Practical Theology at the University of Edinburgh. His publications include *Theology on the menu: Asceticism, meat and Christian diet* (2010).

Heather Lynch was working as a social worker within a criminal justice service for women in central Scotland when she contributed to this volume. She is now undertaking a PhD in Social Work at Glasgow Caledonian University, where her interests include subjectivity and difference.

Malcolm Payne is a writer on social work and end-of-life care, and Honorary Professor at Kingston University, London and Emeritus Professor at Manchester Metropolitan University. His most recent book is *Modern social work theory* (2014).

Mark Smith is a Senior Lecturer and current Head of Social Work at the University of Edinburgh. He has an interest in abuse allegations made against care staff and is currently working on an ESRC-funded project centred on allegations against the former BBC disc jockey, Jimmy Savile. One of his recent books is *Residential child care in practice: Making a difference* (2013), written with Leon Fulcher and Peter Doran.

Series editors' preface

Viviene E. Cree, Gary Clapton and Mark Smith

This book series begins and ends with a question: how useful are ideas of moral panic to the social issues and anxieties that confront us today? Forty years on from the publication of Stan Cohen's seminal study *Folk Devils and Moral Panics*, does this remain a helpful way of thinking about social concerns, or should the concept be consigned to the sociological history books as an amusing, but ultimately flawed, theoretical device? 'Moral panic' is, after all, one of the foremost sociological terms that has crossed over from academic to public discourse; in doing so, it has lost a great deal of its rigour and, arguably, its value. All the contributors to the series are, in their own ways, engaging critically with the relevance of moral panic ideas for their own understandings of some of the most pressing personal, professional and political concerns of the day. They do not all come up with the same conclusions, but they do agree that moral panics – no matter how we think of them – focus on the social issues that worry us most.

The book series takes forward findings from an Economic and Social Research Council (ESRC) sponsored research seminar series that ran between 2012 and 2014 at events across the UK. The seminar series was designed to mark the 40th anniversary of *Folk Devils and Moral Panics*; and to bring together international and UK academics, researchers and practitioners from a range of disciplines to debate and discuss moral panics in the 21st century. The three main organisers had, independently of one another, written about events and happenings that had caused great anxiety within social work and within society as a whole: satanic abuse (Clapton, 1993); sex trafficking (Cree, 2008); abuse in residential childcare (Smith, 2008 and 2010). In each case, we had challenged accepted accounts of the issues and asked questions about the real-life (often negative) consequences of holding particular conceptualisations of these difficult topics. We had not, at that time, used the concept of moral panic as the foremost tool for analysis, but we had all been interested in the ideas of discourse, labelling, deviancy amplification and social control, all of which connect with ideas of moral panic. With the 40th anniversary imminent, we saw this as offering an opportunity to revisit this, asking: what relevance does the idea of moral panic have for an examination of 21st-century social issues and anxieties?

The seminar series produced a number of outcomes: articles, blogs and the collection of papers included in these bytes. However, the collection is broader than the seminar series in two key ways: firstly, some chapters were especially commissioned because it was felt that there was a gap in the collection or because the writer had a particularly interesting approach to the issues; secondly, each of the books in this series ends with an afterword written by a social work practitioner who has been invited to reflect on the contributions from the perspective of practice. This demonstrates not only our commitment to knowledge exchange more generally, but also our belief that moral panic ideas have special relevance for social work.

Moral panics and social work

Although 'moral panic' is a sociological idea that has widespread intellectual interest, it has, as Cohen (1998) acknowledges, special relevance for social work. Social work as an academic discipline and a profession plays a central role in the process of defining social issues and then trying to do something about them – that is our job! So we have to be particularly alert to the part we play within this. We are, in moral panic parlance, 'moral entrepreneurs' and 'claims makers': we tell society (government, policy makers, other practitioners, members of the public) what the social problems are, how they should be understood and how they should be addressed. We do so, in 21st-century terms, through secular, professional and academic discourse, but at heart, what we are expressing is a set of ideas about how we should live and what it is to be human. In other words, we remain a 'moral' and, at times, moralising profession.

The concept of moral panic reminds us that our deeply held attitudes and values have origins and consequences in the real world, both positive and negative. And sometimes they are not the origins or consequences we expect them to be. Hence the lens of moral panic highlights the ways in which social issues that begin with real concerns may lead to the labelling and stigmatising of certain behaviours and individuals; they may precipitate harsh and disproportionate legislation; they may make people more fearful and society a less safe place. Focusing on some social issues may distract attention away from other, underlying concerns; so a focus on trafficking may, for example, ignore the realities of repressive, racist immigration policies, just as a focus on internet pornography may lead to legislation that undermines individual freedom, and a focus on child protection may inhibit our capacity to support families, as Featherstone et al (2014) have identified. These are not issues about which we, as editors and contributors to this series, have answers – but we do have questions. And it is our firm belief that social work must engage with these questions if we are to practise in ways that are truly emancipatory and in line with the social work profession's social justice principles.

A particular moment in the history of moral panics?

The years 2013 and 2014 have proved to be a very particular time in the history of moral panics for two, very different, reasons. The first reason is that a number of key protagonists from the early theoretical writing on deviance, moral panics and the state died in 2013 and early 2014.

- Stan Cohen, sociologist and author of *Folk Devils and Moral Panics* (1972), *Visions of Social Control* (1985), *States of Denial* (2001) and numerous other publications, died in January 2013.
- Geoffrey Pearson, social work professor and author of *The Deviant Imagination* (1975) and *Hooligan: A History of Respectable Fears* (1983), died in April 2013.

- Jock Young, criminologist and author of *The Drugtakers* (1971) and many other studies including, most recently, *The Criminological Imagination* (2011), died in November 2013.
- Stuart Hall, critical theorist, founding editor of *New Left Review* and author with Charles Critcher and others of *Policing the Crisis* (1978), died in February 2014.

We wished to mark the contribution of these great thinkers, and so we have included a commentary on one of them within each byte in the series. This is not to suggest that they are the only people who have written about contemporary social issues in this way; in fact, Geoffrey Pearson was more concerned with the persistent nature of what he called 'respectable discontents' than about the sporadic eruptions of moral panics. But, as the series will demonstrate, theorists from a wide range of academic disciplines have continued to engage with the concept of moral panics over the 40-plus years since 1972, sometimes arguing for its continuing value (for example, Goode and Ben-Yehuda, 1994) and at other times favouring alternative explanations, such as those around risk (for example, Beck, 1992, 1999) and moral regulation (for example, Hunt, 1999). More recently, scholars have attempted to move 'beyond the heuristic', to develop a way of thinking about moral panic that both informs, and continues 'to be informed by, movements and developments in social theory' (Rohloff and Wright, 2010, p 419).

The second reason why this has been a special time is because of what has been called the 'Jimmy Savile effect' in numerous press and media reports. It is difficult to discuss the scandal around Jimmy Savile, TV presenter and prolific sex offender, who died in October 2011, in a dispassionate way. In September and October 2012, almost a year after his death, claims emerged that Savile had committed sexual abuse over many years, with his victims ranging from girls and boys to adults. By October 2012, allegations had been made to 13 British police forces, and a series of inquiries followed. The revelations around the Jimmy Savile affair encouraged others to come forward and claim that they had been abused by celebrities: Stuart Hall (TV presenter, not critical theorist), Rolf Harris, Max Clifford and many others have been investigated and prosecuted. These events have encouraged us to ask wider questions in articles and blogs about physical and sexual abuse, and about potentially negative fall-out from the furore around historic abuse. This has not been easy: how do we get across the reality that we are not minimising the damage that abuse can cause, while at the same time calling for a more questioning approach to victimisation and social control? These questions remain challenging as we move forward.

The series

This series of bytes introduces a collection of papers that engage with a social issue through the lens of moral panic. It will be evident from the chapters that, as editors, we have not imposed a 'moral panic straightjacket' on the contributors; nor do we hold to the notion that there is one 'Moral Panic Theory' with a capital T. Instead, contributors have been invited to consider moral panic ideas very broadly, focusing on their capacity to add to a deeper understanding of the social problem under discussion. Because of this, the series offers a number of opportunities for those who are already familiar with the concept of moral panic and for those who are not. For those who have been thinking about moral panic ideas for years, the series will serve as a new 'take' on some of the puzzling aspects of moral panic theories. For those who are coming across the notion of moral panic for the first time, or have only everyday knowledge of it, the case-study examples of particular social issues and anxieties contained in each chapter will serve as an introduction not only to moral panic as a theoretical concept, but also to what, we hope, might become a new avenue of critical inquiry for readers in the future.

The series is divided into four short volumes ('bytes'): *Gender and family*; *Childhood and youth*; *The state*; and *Moral regulation*. Each byte contains an introduction, which includes a short retrospective on one of the four early theorists whom we have already identified. Five chapters follow, each exploring the case study of one social issue, asking how useful a moral panic lens is (or is not) to understanding this social problem. Each byte ends with an afterword written by a social work practitioner. The four bytes are also available as a single volume – *Revisiting moral panics*, featuring an introduction to Moral Panic Theory by Charles Critcher – with the aim of reaching as wide an audience as possible.

The books in this series should be read as an opening conversation. We are not seeking either consensus or closure in publishing this series; quite the opposite, our aim is to ask questions – of social problems, of professional practice and of ourselves. In doing so, we pay homage to Cohen's (1998, p 112) challenge to 'stay unfinished'; instead of seeking to resolve the contradictions and complexities that plague theory and practice, we must, he argues, be able to live with ambiguity. The series may help us and others to do just that, and, in doing so, may contribute towards the building of a more tolerant, open social work practice and a more tolerant, open society.

Acknowledgement
With thanks to the ESRC for funding the seminar series 'Revisiting Moral Panics: A Critical Examination of 21st Century Social Issues and Anxieties' (ES/J021725/1) between October 2012 and October 2014.

References
Beck, U. (1992) *Risk society: Towards a new modernity*, London: Sage.

Beck, U. (1999) *World risk society*, Cambridge: Polity Press.

Clapton, G. (1993) *Satanic abuse controversy: Social workers and the social work press*, London: University of North London Press.

Cohen, S. (1972) *Folk devils and moral panics: The creation of the mods and rockers*, London: MacGibbon and Kee Ltd.

Cohen, S. (1985) *Visions of social control: Crime, punishment and classification*, Cambridge: Polity Press.

Cohen, S. (1998) *Against criminology,* London: Transaction Publishers.

Cohen, S. (2001) *States of denial knowing about atrocities and suffering*, Cambridge: Polity Press.

Cree, V.E. (2008) 'Confronting sex-trafficking: lessons from history', *International Social Work*, vol 51, no 6, pp 763–76.

Featherstone, B., White, S. and Morris, K. (2014) *Re-imagining child protection: Towards humane social work with families*, Bristol: Policy Press.

Goode, E. and Ben-Yehuda, N. (1994) *Moral panics: The Social construction of deviance*, Oxford: Blackwell.

Hall, S., Critcher, C., Jefferson, T., Clarke, J. and Roberts, B. (1978) *Policing the crisis: Mugging, the state and law and order*, London: Macmillan.

Hunt, A. (1999) *Governing morals: A social history of moral regulation*, Cambridge University Press, New York.

Pearson, G. (1975) *The deviant imagination: Psychiatry, social work and social change*, London: Macmillan.

Pearson, G. (1983) *Hooligan: A history of respectable fears,* London: Macmillan.

Rohloff, A. and Wright, S. (2010) 'Moral panic and social theory: beyond the heuristic', *Current Sociology*, vol 58, no 3, pp 403–19.

Smith, M. (2008) 'Historical abuse in residential child care: an alternative view', *Practice: Social Work in Action*, vol 20, no 1, pp 29–41.

Smith, M. (2010) 'Victim narratives of historical abuse in residential child care: do we really know what we think we know?', *Qualitative Social Work*, vol 9, no 3, pp 303–20.

Young, J. (1971) *The drugtakers: The social meaning of drug use*, London: Paladin.

Young, J. (2011) *The criminological imagination*, Cambridge: Polity Press.

Introduction

Mark Smith

This byte introduces another key theorist within the moral panic genre. The work of Jock Young has played a central part in the creation of ideas around moral panic, and these, as will be shown, have developed over time. Some of Young's ideas are reflected in the chapters here and the preceding bytes in the series, while others have been taken forward in other writing in the field.

Jock Young

Jock Young was born William Young on 4 March 1942 in Vogrie, Midlothian. When he was five, his family moved to Aldershot, where his Scottish background led to his being given the nickname Jock, which stuck throughout his adult life. Young studied sociology at the London School of Economics. He co-founded the first National Deviancy Conference (NDC) in 1968, where he presented his first conference paper, 'The Role of Police as Amplifiers of Deviancy'. This idea of deviancy amplification was developed in his first major work, *The Drugtakers* (1971). It was this book that introduced the concept of 'moral panic' into sociological literature, not Cohen's (1972) *Folk Devils and Moral Panics* as is commonly thought.

Young moved to Middlesex Polytechnic (now Middlesex University) in the 1980s and headed up the Centre for Criminology there. He remained at Middlesex for 35 years before moving to the City University of New York in 2002, and later to the University of Kent. In 2009, he returned to New York as Professor of Criminal Justice and Sociology at the City University of New York Graduate Center.

Young is recognised as one of the world's pre-eminent criminologists. His perspective shifted from a radical, critical one to arguing for a more engaged 'left realist' criminology, which asserted that law and order was a socialist issue and that the victims of crime are predominantly the poor and the marginalised. His left realist approach was to some extent adopted by the UK Labour Party in its slogan 'Tough on crime, tough on the causes of crime', although Young became disillusioned that New Labour tended to underplay the second part of this equation. Throughout his life and work, he maintained a radical and critical edge.

Intellectually, Young was a sociologist in the tradition of C. Wright Mills. His book *The Criminological Imagination* (2011) acknowledges Mills's legacy and critiques the positivist, abstracted empiricism and the lack of imagination in much current-day criminology. *The Criminological Imagination* and *The Vertigo of Late Modernity* (2007) are both based on an analysis of the cultural shifts associated with late modernity. Young's work draws extensively on contemporary issues to make and support his arguments. It was in *The Vertigo of Late Modernity* that he developed more fully his ideas about moral panic. Here he argues that it is a sense of insecurity that provides the conditions for moral panic to emerge and take hold. He describes moral panics as moral disturbances 'centring on claims that direct interests have been violated'. They are 'not simply panics, media generated or otherwise that provide false information'. Moral disturbance is characterised by a feeling of anxiety; in that sense, it is real, and cannot be readily dismissed as irrational. Moral panics take personal anxiety to a societal level; they do not occur when political and social structures are solid and successful but, rather, when they are in crisis, when society's tectonic plates are shifting. Young goes on to argue that when societies are in crisis, personal and social unease is displaced onto a scapegoat; scapegoated groups are not chosen by accident, but are closely related to the source of anxiety. The denigration of the 'other' creates the conditions for constituting a demon or folk devil; the folk devil in any culture is 'that it is what they are not' (Young, 2007, p 141).

Importantly for this byte, Young's work, reflecting Wright Mills's influence, synthesises the structural with the personal and, in so doing, offers compelling insights into the moral dimension of the human condition.

Jock Young died on 16 November 2013.

Content of this byte

Moral regulation brings together chapters around what might, on the surface, appear to be rather disparate subject matter. Some common themes emerge, however, to provide compelling illustrations of many of the elements of Jock Young's thesis. Perhaps, the most obvious message is that moral panics are likely to erupt around issues of profound moral importance (but also where there is a perceived threat), such as life and death, good and evil, sex (especially when linked with children), the body and an existential threat to cherished beliefs and institutions.

In Chapter One Frank Furedi identifies the folk devil par excellence of the late modern period, the paedophile, personified in recent times in the figure of Jimmy Savile. The paedophile is counter-posed with the sacralised child, who emerges as a rare focus of moral consensus in an uncertain world. Furedi questions whether the term moral panic, which in most instances would run its course before petering out, is sufficient to capture the enduring nature of our fears around children or whether 'permanent panic' or 'crusade' might more accurately reflect the staying power of the paedophilia narrative.

In Chapter Two David Grumett provides a fascinating case study of a Danish ban on the slaughter of farm animals without pre-stunning. The ban was enacted in 2014, yet the last abattoir performing such killings closed 10 years previously. A heated debate emerged nevertheless, bringing to the surface some of the visceral (literally) feelings that questions of food and its ingestion into the body can give rise to. While Jock Young identifies how moral entrepreneurs might claim scientific 'evidence' to afford some provenance to their cases, Grummett suggests that, in this case, some rudimentary scientific and technical understanding would have been useful in bringing some sense of perspective to the issue.

Michaela Benson and Katharine Charsley address the panic in the UK around supposedly sham marriages in Chapter Three. Like Grumett (and indeed, this is a point that Jock Young picked up in *The Vertigo of Late Modernity*), they identify the 'othering' of non-western cultures that emerges in this instance over a perceived threat to the 'cherished' institution of marriage. Thus, 'sham' marriages are seen as loveless and entered into for an ulterior purpose – presumably counterposed with loving and nurturing qualities in western marriages. The ambiguity and ontological uncertainty betrayed by such a view in a context of declining use or stability of marriage in the West scarcely needs to be pointed out.

Colin Clark in Chapter Four continues this theme of ethnic scapegoating, drawing on his own research into the Roma community in Glasgow. Hostility to Roma people worldwide was fuelled and reified by the case of Maria, the young girl at the centre of an alleged child abduction by virtue of the fact that she had different colouring to her parents. This case, again, crystalises the essentialising features of moral panics, totalising what is in fact a heterogeneous Roma population into an undifferentiated but threatening mass. Clark draws on sociological and anthropological perspectives, alluding in particular to Mary Douglas's work on dirt and pollution to cast light on tendencies to characterise Roma sanitation and rubbish disposal behaviours. What is missing, of course, in this discourse is any appreciation that, in a context of austerity, Roma people may have moved to Britain to improve their prospects, engage in a variety of employment practices and raise their children.

Malcolm Payne's Chapter Five is slightly different in that although his subject matter addresses the deeply ontological issue of death and assisted dying, where strongly held views are brought to bear, it is hard to discern any real panic in the way that the issue has played out in the public domain. Rather, a moral question is subject to moral debate in which competing viewpoints are articulated and contested. One is left to speculate why an issue that could have lent itself to panic has not done so but, in many respects, offers an example of how emotionally charged and contested subject matter might be properly engaged with. As David Grumett notes, 'In any case, moral panic is a poor substitute for serious moral debate or argument'.

References

Cohen, S. (1972) *Folk devils and moral panics*, London: MacGibbon and Kee Ltd.

Mills, C.W. (1959) *The sociological imagination*, Oxford: Oxford University Press.

Young, J. (1971) *The drugtakers: The social meaning of drug use*, London: MacGibbon and Kee.

Young, J. (2007) *The vertigo of late modernity*, London: Sage.

Young, J. (2011) *The criminological imagination*, Cambridge: Polity.

ONE

The moral crusade against paedophilia

Frank Furedi

Introduction

The focus of this essay is the transformation of the threat of paedophilia into a permanent focus of moral outrage. It explores the moral landscape that has turned the child predator into the principal target of moral enterprise. Through a discussion of the concept of a moral crusade it evaluates the impact of society's obsessive preoccupation with the child predator.

Paedophilia and the threat it represents to children has become a permanent feature of public concern and a regular theme of popular culture. The paedophile personifies evil in 21st-century society; the child predator possesses the stand-alone status of the embodiment of malevolence. But this unique personification of evil is not an isolated figure hovering on the margins of 21st-century society. Jimmy Savile, who died in 2011 and who has not been out of the news during the past two years, was dubbed the most 'prolific' paedophile in British history. What is unique about the activities of this alleged celebrity predator is the scale of his operation rather than his behaviour. Allegations against Savile effortlessly acquired the status of a cultural truth, since it is widely believed that, rather than rare, the abuse of children is a very common activity.

According to the cultural script of virtually every western society, child abusers are ubiquitous. This script invites the public to regard all strangers – particularly men – as potential child molesters. The concept of 'stranger danger' and the campaigns that promote it have as their explicit objective the educating of children to mistrust adults that they do not know. This narrative of stranger danger helps to turn what ought to be the unthinkable into an omnipresent threat that preys on our imagination. Represented as a universal threat, the peril of paedophilia demands perpetual vigilance. The expectation that adult strangers represent a risk to children has in effect turned concern about paedophilia into a very normal feature of life. That is why physical contact between adults and children has become so intensely scrutinised and policed.

'I think what is absolutely horrific, frankly, is the extent to which this child abuse has been taking place over the years and across our communities over the years', stated Theresa May, the UK Secretary of State for Home Affairs, when she outlined the details of the government's inquiry into sexual abuse in North Wales care homes and into Jimmy Savile's activities (see Theresa May, quoted by Nigel Morris in the *Independent* [Morris, 2012]). Her insistence on the all-pervasive character of child abuse resonates with widespread anxiety about the scourge of paedophilia. In official discourse this threat is expressed in a uniquely unrestrained and dramatic manner. Moral entrepreneurs, especially those associated with the child-protection industry, adopt a rhetoric that is classically associated with scaremongering demonologists. They continually use the discourse of big numbers to support the argument that 'all children are at risk'. England's Deputy Children's Commissioner, Sue Berelowitz, demonstrated this when she declared that 'there isn't a town, village or hamlet in which children are not being sexually exploited' (see Berelowitz, quoted by Graeme Wilson, in *The Sun* [Wilson, 2012]). The moral weight of such claims is rarely contested, since anyone who questions the doctrine of the omnipresence of abuse is likely to be denounced as an appeaser of the child predator.

An ideology of evil

The narrative of paedophilia does not merely encompass the abuse of children. It has become a free-floating idiom of fear that can attach itself to any focus of anxiety. So when the Southern Baptist leader Reverend

Jerry Vines declared in June 2002 that Mohammed was a 'demon possessed paedophile' and that Allah leads Muslims to terrorism, he was merely harnessing the power of this idiom of fear to promote his apocalyptic vision of the future of the world (Sachs, 2002). It is not just religious fundamentalists who allow their fantasies about paedophiles to intermesh with their wider perceptions of global insecurity. It was announced in 2014 that as far as the British government is concerned, it would like to treat paedophiles in the same way as terrorists. It was reported that Prime Minister David Cameron was determined to close a 'loophole' that permits paedophiles to publish and possess 'manuals' that offer tips to would-be child predators about how to identify and groom their targets. Cameron indicated that such a new law would authorise the British state to apply the same kind of extraordinary sanctions used to target terrorists who download bomb-making manuals (Hope, 2014).

The adoption of the tactics and strategy of the war against terrorism to the crusade against paedophiles is symptomatic of a world-view that risks losing the capacity to understand the distinction between fantasy and reality. The merging of the threat of the violent terrorist with that of the online predator dramatises the threat of both. Imperceptibly, the terrorist network and the ring of paedophiles become indistinguishable from one another and, through the rhetorical act of joined-up scaremongering, this meshing intensifies the public's sense of insecurity.

From the standpoint of cultural sociology, what is particularly interesting is the transformation of paedophilia into an idiom of evil, one that serves as a moral resource for competing claims makers to draw on. Since the early 1980s, Britain and many other societies have experienced a succession of highly charged alarmist outbursts over paedophile-related incidents. Such incidents have led to mob violence against individuals wrongly accused of child abuse and to the killing of individuals who were victims of mistaken identity. Even the most improbable claims (such as scaremongering allegations of satanic ritual abuse (SRA)) have been treated as if they were based on hard evidence and facts. More than three decades of recurrent panics about the threat of paedophilia have had the cumulative impact of transforming the periodic outburst of anxiety over specific cases of abuse into a stable outlook through which communities make sense of the uncertainties of daily life.

The normalisation of paedophilia as an existential threat haunting childhood provides a rare example of the mutation of what first emerged as a moral panic in the 1980s into a coherent and enduring ideology of evil. That this ideology exercises influence over society is demonstrated by the fact that childhood and relations between generations have been regularly reorganised to contain the peril of paedophilia. Consequently, relations between generations are now carefully regulated and policed. In every walk of life, an assumption of 'guilty until proven innocent' underpins intergenerational relations. The premise that all adults pose a potential risk to children means that the criminal records check is the current index of trust; police checks on millions of adults are deemed essential before they can be trusted to be near, or to work with, children.

Experience indicates that suspicion towards adult motives only begets more mistrust. Numerous informal rules have been introduced to prevent adults from coming into direct physical contact with children. Even nursery workers feel that their action is under constant scrutiny. Adult carers have not been entirely banned from applying sun cream on children. Some still follow their human instinct and do what they believe is in the best interest of a child. But frequently, this practice requires formal parental consent. It is now common practice for nurseries and schools to send out letters to parents to sign to give teachers the right to put sun cream on their child. Some nurseries have sought to get around this problem by asking their employees to use sprays rather than rub sun cream onto children's bodies. These 'no touch' rules are underpinned by an ideology that regards physical contact between adults and children as a precursor to potentially malevolent behaviour (see Piper and Stronach, 2008).

Bans in one domain of adult–child interaction have a nasty habit of leading to bans in another. 'No-touch' rules are followed by 'no picture' rules that seek to prevent parents and others from taking pictures of children during school plays, concerts and sporting activity. In some playgrounds and parks, there are rules that seek to ban 'unaccompanied adults' from entering the site. From this perspective, the idea that an adult watching a child play can be an innocent act of enjoying the sight of youngsters fooling around is simply preposterous; only a pervert, it is suggested, would wish to watch other people's children playing.

The proliferation of rules governing intergenerational relations is underpinned by an ideology of evil. For moral entrepreneurs, society's insecurity about paedophilia strengthens the case for their argument that 'something must be done'. It provides opportunities for moral positioning against the one evil that all of us can agree on. The moral entrepreneur is a rule creator who, explains the sociologist Howard Becker, 'feels that nothing can be right in the world until rules are made to correct it'. However, since evil is omnipresent, every new rule serves only as a prelude to the next. A moral crusader is a 'professional discoverer of wrongs to be righted, of situations requiring new rules' (Becker, 1963, pp 147–8 and 153). Though they are often 'fervent' and 'self-righteous', they are not motivated by cynicism or opportunism, but by the impulse of helping others (Becker, 1963, p 148). They invariably perceive themselves as the champions of suffering victims. However, despite their intentions, zealous crusades often incite confusion and moral disorientation.

From the standpoint of cultural sociology, the numerous campaigns launched to protect children and to promote an alarmist state of concern about the threat of child predators is usefully captured by the concept of a moral crusade. In his classic study of moral enterprise, Becker concludes that the 'final outcome of the moral crusade is a police force' (Becker, 1963, p 156). Threats are represented as not just physical hazards, but a danger to the natural order of things. It was this perception in early modern Europe that gave witch-hunting its mandate and fierce passion. Similarly, the powerful sense of moral repugnance of the practice of 'self-pollution' by 18th-century moral entrepreneurs against the dangers of masturbation was inextricably linked to the conviction that this was the most unnatural of acts. Advocates of these causes almost effortlessly make the conceptual jump from unnatural to malevolent and from malevolent to evil.

Contemporary society is not usually comfortable with the moral condemnation of evil. Indeed 21st-century western culture is estranged from a grammar of morality. Consequently, with the notable exception of sexual abuse, threats and dangers are rarely conveyed in an explicit moral form. Moral regulation often possesses an incoherent form and may be promoted indirectly through the language of health, science and risks. Fear appeals frequently appear as a response to non-moral and scientifically affirmed objective imperatives; such appeals directed against smoking are paradigmatic in this respect (see Thompson et al, 2009).

The disassociation of objects of dread and fear from the grammar of morality does not mean that warnings about them have been denuded of the imperative of moralisation. What it signifies is that the contemporary culture of fear makes it difficult to draw on the authority of an uncontested moral code. That is why paedophilia has such a culturally strategic significance. Paedophilia, along with a small number of inter-personal abuses, has a formidable capacity to incite moral outrage. What endows paedophilia with a unique quality to excite alarm and consternation is that it appears to represent the annihilation of childhood. And if the paedophile is the personification of evil, then the child has become a symbol of its moral opposite. Some social scientists believe that a sublimated form of guilt accounts for the intense hostility towards the child molester. Garland (2008, p 17) wrote that 'the intensity of current fear and loathing of child abusers seems to be connected to unconscious guilt about negligent parenting and widespread ambivalence about the sexualisation of modern culture'.

In the name of the child

The sacralisation of the child is the flip side of the tendency to universalise the threat of paedophilia. The unique moral status of the sacred child is so powerful that it is literally beyond discussion. As Anneke Meyer observes, '"the child" becomes a shorthand for sacralisation and moral status; its meaning no longer has to be made explicit'. She concludes that this narrative is 'so powerful that in fact *any* opinion can be justified by simply referring to children, and without having to explain *why* and *how* children justify it'. The very mention of the word 'children' closes down discussion; the discourse on the perils of childhood provides an uncontested validation for claims making and '*anything* can be justified via children as children make the case good and right' (Meyer, 2007, p 60).

Fear appeals that manipulate our natural anxiety towards children are actively promoted to encourage a disposition towards suspicion and mistrust. Mention the word 'child' and people will listen. Raise the moral stakes by claiming that a 'child is at risk' and people will not just listen but endorse your demand that 'something must be done'. Consequently campaigners against poverty understand that they are far more likely to gain sympathy for their cause by focusing attention on what is now called 'child poverty'. Abstract socioeconomic injustices gain compelling definition through recasting poverty as an affliction confronting a child. Campaigners on Third World issues know that the very mention of 'child labour' or the 'exploitation of children' or 'child soldiers' or 'starving children' is far more likely to resonate with a western public than calls for economic assistance. In education a call for 'child centred' teaching will gain you a standing ovation. 'Mention the word children, and the money rolls in', remarks an acquaintance who works as a fund-raising consultant in the charity sector.

Children serve as a moral resource with which to promote policies and causes. The tendency on the part of moral entrepreneurs to hide behind the child and frame their message through the narrative of child protection is motivated by the recognition that it is a uniquely effective communication strategy. The cause of child protection enjoys formidable cultural support. Indeed the child has emerged as a very rare focus for moral consensus. As I argue elsewhere, in a world of existential disorientation the child serves as the main focus for both emotional and moral investment (Furedi, 2008). The sacralisation of the child means that those who speak 'in the name of the child' can benefit from the moral resources associated with children. At a time when society finds it difficult to express itself through the grammar of morality and where there are big disputes about what is right and wrong, the child stands out as a singular exemplar of moral unity. People may argue about whether gay marriage is right or wrong. They may dispute the legitimacy of assisted suicide, the right to abortion or the desirability of sex education. But all sides of the debate are unequivocally for the sacred child. That is also why in the current age paedophilia has emerged as most powerful symbol of evil.

Using children as a moral shield is now widely practised by policy makers and fear entrepreneurs. They understand that most adults find it difficult to raise their doubts about the numerous policies that are promoted through their alleged benefit for the security of children. Civil rights campaigners against identity cards and numerous attempts to expand government surveillance tend to lose their voice when children are brought into the discussion. So there was virtually no criticism raised by the announcement by the current England and Wales Health Services Minister, Dan Poulter, that, starting in 2015, all children who visit an accident and emergency (A&E) department in a hospital will be logged on a new national database set up to identify potential victims of abuse (*Belfast Telegraph*, 2012). It appears that when the word child is mentioned, then surveillance and the loss of doctor and patient confidentiality are acceptable. Similarly, campaigners who are usually vigilant about encroachment on civil liberties when it comes to new anti-terrorism laws have appeared indifferent to the vetting of millions of adults under different schemes designed to police those who work with or come into contact with children.

The moral crusade

Since the 1970s, social scientists have frequently characterised periodic outbursts of outrage and anxiety as a moral panic. This is a concept that appears to capture the anger and outrage precipitated by the many examples of public scandals during the four decades since that time. One of the strengths of the original conceptualisation of the concept of moral panic was that it drew attention to the important moral dimension of society's reaction to and perception of a problem. However, in the absence of moral consensus such reactions often self-consciously avoid using a moral language to express their cause. For example, at least in public, anti-abortionists often prefer using a medical vocabulary warning of psychological damage and trauma, rather than to use the language of evil and sin: the assertion that 'abortion is bad' is replaced by the argument that 'abortion is bad for *you*'. This shift in the way that threats to society are represented has important implications for the relevance of moral panic theory. David Garland (2008, p 17) points to 'a shift *away* from moral panics' in societies like the UK and the US, 'where it is difficult to find any public issue on which there is broad public agreement and an absence of dissenting voices'. At a time when competing lifestyles and attitudes towards personal behaviour are the subject of acrimonious debate, it is rare for different sections of society to unite against traditional folk devils.

There are, of course, issues that provoke a solid moral consensus and in those circumstances it is appropriate to use the concept of moral panics. Garland (2008, p 17) believes that in America the 'panic over child abuse' is an example of a 'genuine moral panic'. The same observation holds for Britain and most western societies. As already stated, panics about paedophilia have a unique capacity to mobilise powerful emotions and harness the moral sentiments of the entire public. However, given the durability of this reaction and its institutionalisation, the term 'panic' may no longer capture the features of what has crystallised into a fairly permanent outlook on life. Possibly the term 'permanent panic' provides a more suggestive term through which attention can be drawn to the stable, durable and all-pervasive character of this phenomenon.

There are, of course, historical precedents for moral panics to transform into a relatively stable and durable outlook on the world. In the late 14th century, moral anxiety about the practice of witchcraft mutated into a demonology focused on the threat posed by satanic forces. Through the energetic efforts of anti-witchcraft campaigners, European society came to imagine and fear a secret dark power that could destroy the life of anyone in any community. The life span of most scares can be measured in months, years and sometimes decades. But the fear of witchcraft haunted communities for centuries. With different degrees of intensity it influenced people's behaviour from the late 14th to the middle of the 17th century. It was through the promotion of the dread of witchcraft that modern scaremongering really came into its own. Until the 19th century, and arguably even today, the fear of witchcraft can readily incite people to panic and behave in a cruel and destructive manner.

The legacy of pre-modern witch-hunting actually influences present-day anti-paedophile demonology. In Britain, scaremongering about satanic abuse gained respectability when the National Society for the Prevention of Cruelty to Children published its 'Satanic indicators' to assist social workers to recognise the likely profile of a Satanist. Sadly, many professionals were convinced that organised groups of Satanists were preying on youngsters, and numerous children were taken into care. A network of child protection 'experts', therapists and social workers played a key role in promoting the idea that SRA was a significant threat to British children. Nottinghamshire Social Services department played a leading role in promoting the crusade against Satanist child abusers. It helped to launch RAINS (Ritual Abuse Information and Network and Support), an organisation designed to publicise the danger from Satanists. In the end, a series of inquiries concluded that claims of SRA made by Nottinghamshire Social Services were without substance. One report written, by J.B. Gwatkin, warned that if the crusade was not stopped 'there was the likelihood of a "witch-hunt" which would result in grave injustice to children and their abuse by professional staff' (see Gwatkin, 1997)). No one was burned at the stake for SRA. But numerous families faced a nightmare as their lives were destroyed by zealous witch-hunters who took their children away. Others faced long jail sentences for crimes that were figments of the scaremongers' imagination. And although many of the legal proceedings failed to make the charges stick, there were many innocent parents who were 'framed' for a crime that they had not committed and did not exist.

Hopefully, the demonology that surrounds the child predator will not have the staying power of its distinguished medieval predecessor. Why? Because throughout history, the security of children has relied on adults assuming responsibility for their welfare. The mistrust that now envelops intergenerational relations threatens to discourage many adults from assuming this responsibility. Indeed, there is now a generation of adults who have acquired the habit of distancing themselves from children and young people. Moral crusaders, whatever their intentions, have helped to create a world where many adults regard intergenerational relations as an inconvenience from which they would rather be exempt. Arguably, the disengagement of many adults from the world of children represents a far greater danger than the threat posed by a (thankfully) tiny group of predators. The best guarantee of children's safety is the exercise of adult responsibility towards the younger generation. It is when adults take it on themselves to keep an eye on children – and not just simply their own – that youngsters can learn to feel genuinely safe.

Our examination of this long-standing moral crusade leads to the conclusion that society's reaction to the threat of the child predator is different to that of 'normal' moral panics. What began as the periodic outburst of panic has mutated into a constant regime of vigilance. This threat, *sui generis* has become a recurrent theme in the cultural imagination of society. The spectre of the paedophile that constantly haunts society is continually brought to the attention of the public by moral entrepreneurs. The significant moral capital invested in this symbol of evil ensures that the crusades against it are likely to continue into the future. Arguably, the permanent moral crusade against paedophilia bears comparison with the targeting of witchcraft in the early modern era.

References

Becker, H.S. (1963) *Outsiders. Studies in the sociology of deviance*, New York: The Free Press.

Belfast Telegraph (2012) 'Child medical visits to be logged', 27 December, http://article.wn.com/view/2012/12/27/Child_medical_visits_to_be_logged/ (accessed 17 March 2015).

Furedi, F. (2008) *Paranoid parenting*, London: Continuum Press.

Garland, D. (2008) 'The concept of a moral panic', *Crime Media Culture*, vol 4, no 1, pp 9–30.

Gwatkin, J.B. (1997) 'Introduction', The Broxtowe Files, www.users.globalnet.co.uk/~dlheb/introduc.htm (accessed 8 February 2015).

Hope, C. (2014) 'Cameron to close legal loophole that lets paedophiles download child grooming manuals', *Telegraph* (27 April), www.telegraph.co.uk/news/politics/10791387/Cameron-to-close-legal-loophole-that-lets-paedophiles-download-child-grooming-manuals.html (accessed 17 March 2015).

Meyer, A. (2007) *The child at risk: Paedophiles, media responses and public opinion*, Manchester: Manchester University Press.

Morris, N. (2012) 'Theresa May calls extent of paedophile activity across Britain "absolutely horrific"', *Independent* (6 November), www.independent.co.uk/news/uk/politics/theresa-may-calls-extent-of-paedophile-activity-across-britain-absolutely-horrific-8289526.html

Piper, H. and Stronach, I. (2008) *Don't Touch! The educational story of a panic*, London: Routledge.

Sachs, S. (2002) 'Baptist pastor attacks Islam, inciting cries of intolerance', www.nytimes.com/2002/06/15/national/15BAPT.html (accessed 8 February 20150.

Thompson, L.E., Barnett, J.R. and Pearce, J.R. (2009) 'Scared straight? Fear appeal anti-smoking campaigns, risk, self efficacy and addiction', *Health, Risk and Society*, vol 11, no 2, pp 181–96.

Wilson, G. (2012) 'There isn't a town, village or hamlet in which children are not being sexually exploited', *The Sun* (13 June), www.thesun.co.uk/sol/homepage/news/politics/4369516/There-isnt-a-town-village-or-hamlet-in-which-children-are-not-being-sexually-exploited-MPs-are-told-thousands-of-girls-are-being-raped-by-gangs-across-the-whole-of-Britain.html

TWO

Animal welfare, morals and faith in the 'religious slaughter' debate

David Grumett

Much of the discourse on contemporary 'moral panics' has evolved within the fields of social work and social policy, with obvious examples including child abuse, urban crime, youth culture and immigration. In this chapter, however, a moral panic will be considered centring on the welfare of animals slaughtered for meat according to the requirements of Islam and Judaism.

Introduction

On 17 February 2014, the Danish government banned the slaughter of farm animals without pre-stunning. Denmark thus joined Sweden, Latvia and Poland, the three other European states in which non-stun slaughter is already prohibited (Ferrari and Bottoni, 2010; Anon, 2012). The ban was controversial because some Muslim and many Jewish authorities regard the absence of stunning prior to slaughter as a requirement for the meat to be halal or kosher (which means 'permissible') under Islamic and Jewish law. The resulting public debate differed markedly between countries. In Denmark, it centred on whether the prohibition was compatible with the right of Muslims and Jews to religious freedoms. In practice the ban changed nothing, as no non-stun slaughter had in fact taken place there for a decade. Since the last abattoir licensed to perform it closed in 2004, those of the country's 220,000 Muslims and 8,000 Jews who have wished to consume halal or kosher meat produced without stunning have imported it. Some commentators suggested that the ban, which was obviously associated with animal welfare, was introduced to appease the outrage surrounding the slaughter of a giraffe eight days earlier at Copenhagen Zoo and the public feeding of its carcase to the lion pack. This prior episode had nothing to do with religion.

In the United Kingdom, the Danish ban had the effect of focusing attention onto the absence of any similar prohibition in domestic law. The result was several days of debate that displayed most of the classic features of a moral panic as defined by social theorists such as Cohen (2002) and Thompson (1998, pp 1–30). A campaign quickly developed that was intense even if of brief duration, and the news media played a prominent role in presenting and sustaining it. Strong action was called for, with links made to wider anxieties about social fragmentation or breakdown, in this case due to Islam in Britain. Values and interests, in this case of non-humans, were presented as threatened by an easily identifiable source, while the real issues, both technical and moral, were almost completely ignored.

Background: a distinctive panic

This panic exhibited two interesting features. First was its relation to food. Issues around what is eaten evoke multiple moral anxieties and instinctual responses – 'gut reactions' – due to the intimate nature of the activity of eating. As objects are ingested, physical boundaries are transgressed and bodies rendered potentially impure, whether by inadequate nutritional provision, increased weight or size, or heightened sexual desire. If an issue involves food and eating, it may therefore be more likely that moral panics will develop around it than if it does not involve food (Coveney, 2006). A good example from almost precisely a year earlier was the horsemeat controversy. The primary issues here were the labelling and traceability of meat in a mass market, which are matters of process rather than of morals. Nevertheless, as news about the 'contamination' of beef, pork, lamb and chicken with horsemeat spread, a full moral panic developed – motivated in part by the British unease with the consumption of horseflesh – that exhibited many similar features to the panic around 'religious slaughter'.

The second interesting feature of the moral panic about slaughter, not shared with the horsemeat episode, was its association with Islam. In classic panics, such as those about crime or youth culture, if religion features at all it is presented as a declining moral and social force. Religious decline is thereby linked with wider moral nihilism and societal dissolution. In the panic currently under discussion, however, the absence of any domestic ban on non-stun slaughter led to attention being directed onto the increasing power of Islam in Britain and the allegedly corrosive moral effects of its purportedly barbaric practices. This critique assumes the opposite relation between morals and religion to that standardly presented (for example, Brown, 2009), in which the primary function of religion, especially as practised within the domestic sphere, is to preserve and transmit responsible and humane morals. As Noble (2012, p 215) has argued, recent panics related to Islam have been part of a hardening of the perceived boundaries between good and bad and the construction of Islam as a monolithic 'other' that is morally militant, conservative and fundamentalist. Typically, these panics centre on issues of gender and sexual rights or on terrorism. Where these topics are concerned, Islam is indeed frequently presented as morally militant. However, in the moral panic around slaughter the implication was not that Islam is moralistic but that, at least where animal welfare is concerned, Islam is immoral. Religion was perceived not as supporting morals but as undermining them.

Technical and scientific aspects

The slaughter method employed for halal meat is termed *dhabihah*. Within Great Britain at least 39 slaughterhouses employ this method for sheep and goats, 29 for poultry and 16 for cattle (Food Standards Agency, 2012, p 5).[1] The key welfare debate surrounds recoverable pre-cut stunning, which renders an animal unconscious to pain but does not kill it. The act of killing is the subsequent severing of the carotid arteries, jugular vein and windpipe in the neck. If this were not to take place sufficiently quickly an animal would recover consciousness. In Britain, the Halal Food Authority (HFA) (2014) approves of the electric water-bath stunning of broiler chickens, with research suggesting that electric stunning, if administered at appropriate frequencies, is both effective and recoverable (Wotton et al, 2014). However, there are significant welfare issues with this type of stunning, due to incorrectly calibrated equipment and poor operator training. In particular, the current needs to be varied according to the number of birds on the line, with fine gradations required to deliver a recoverable but effective stun. For lambs and sheep, the HFA also approves of electric-tong stunning. There are fewer welfare problems with this because the animals are stunned individually.

The HFA's approval of electrical stunning is in line with the directions of Islamic authorities in some other Muslim countries, such as Malaysia and Egypt (Salamano et al, 2013, pp 448–9). Moreover, such stunning is required by the two Islamic regulatory authorities in New Zealand, which supplies a global halal market that includes Indonesia and Saudi Arabia (Farouk, 2013, pp 813–15). However, the HFA's approval is disputed by some British Muslims, by the Halal Monitoring Committee UK (HMCUK) (2014) and by most Jews, who regard stunning prior to slaughter as disfiguring an animal and express concern about the pain it causes. Furthermore, for cattle, neither the HFA nor the HMCUK approves captive bolt stunning, which is the standard method used.[2] Nonetheless, at premises licensed to slaughter for halal consumption over 80% of all species, including cattle, are pre-stunned (Food Standards Agency, 2012, p 5). It is unclear where all this meat ends up. Many slaughterhouses serve both religious and non-religious markets, and the HMCUK has expressed concern that meat sold as halal has been pre-stunned.[3] It has instituted a system of regular inspections of abattoirs, caterers and shops, whereas the HFA relies on spot checks.

Turning to kosher meat, the slaughter method employed is termed *shechita*. This requires a clean cut performed with a large, sharp knife. Within the five or so slaughterhouses that use this, post-cut stunning is already carried out on around 10% of cattle (Food Standards Agency, 2012, p 5).[4] Post-cut stunning ensures that even if *shechita* does not render an animal fully unconscious, such a state quickly ensues. Shechita UK (2009 p 8) does not explicitly disapprove of this procedure, circumventing the issue by defining stunning restrictively as the 'methods of attempting to render an animal or bird unconscious prior to slaughter'. This is because approval of post-cut stunning would be a tacit admission that the cut itself does not effectively stun.

A moral panic?

It was clear that most contributors to the debate possessed limited knowledge of the issues. The moral judgements made against slaughter for halal consumption were grounded in an implicitly unfavourable comparison with slaughter for non-halal consumption. However, very few people understand the technical workings of even an ordinary slaughterhouse and the welfare issues these present. For instance, why is the shackling and electric water-bath stunning of broiler chickens still permitted when gas or other controlled-atmosphere systems deliver improved welfare and reliability? Why have many smaller slaughterhouses closed, resulting in animals being transported longer distances for slaughter? Why have older slaughterhouses not been required to be rebuilt in order to deliver high-quality lairage and optimal animal movements through the facility? (Farm Animal Welfare Council, 2009b, pp 142; 2003, pp 19, 48, 53) Issues such as these are prominent in current discussions among experts on welfare at killing and suggest that some practices in and around ordinary slaughterhouses, on which most meat eaters depend, are themselves morally suboptimal. This was not recognised during the moral panic, due to ignorance of the morally relevant facts of normal practice and a lack of interest in finding out about them.

The widespread lack of understanding of these complexities was mirrored, as usual, by terminological confusion. The act of slaughter is often referred to as halal (for Muslims) or kosher (for Jews), but these terms in fact mean 'permissible' or 'lawful' and designate the meat or other food deemed fit for consumption, not the process by which these are produced, nor any part of this process. Strictly, the act of slaughter is referred to as *dhabihah* or *zibah* (by Muslims) or *shechita* (by Jews), as in this chapter. The frequent popular use of the terms 'halal' and 'kosher' to designate the act of slaughter obscures their specifically legal and, by extension, moral meanings, falsely associating them with a purported absence or circumvention of legal regulation or moral reasoning. This can contribute to the denigration of other areas of halal or kosher discipline unrelated to meat.

The necessarily detailed discussion in the previous section of actual slaughter processes and divergences of interpretation between and within religious groups has shown that key to the moral panic was a failure in technical understanding of the issues and a rush to moralise them. This included ignorance of the significant differences between ordinary slaughter and slaughter for the production of meat deemed halal or kosher, as well as a lack of awareness of the divergences of interpretation of the halal and kosher requirements between and within Muslim and Jewish communities. In the panic about slaughter the moral aspect assumed premature prominence and was largely disconnected from the kind of technical and terminological comprehension on which real understanding of any complex applied moral issue depends. This confirms the findings of Noble (2012, p 216) that, at least with regard to Islam, moral panic belies an ability to deal with the 'inescapable heterogeneous and conflictual nature of moral complexity'.

Also identifiable in the panic was critics' projection onto Muslims of uncertainties and anxieties about their own moral decisions and compromises. A large area of moral high ground was rapidly colonised by people who, in most cases, would have been implicated in the incarceration and killing of animals in numbers far exceeding those required for optimal human or planetary flourishing (Maurer and Sobal, 1995). Slaughter for halal and kosher consumption was presented as violent and unnecessary – an assessment that, with some justification, has been made of all animal slaughter by the increasing numbers of people who are reducing their meat consumption or avoiding meat entirely, due to a concern to reduce animal suffering (Spencer, 1993, pp 295–348; Sapontzis, 2004).

Conclusion: from panic to debate

Was the moral panic justified and did it achieve any useful outcomes? The panic was to some extent justified because real welfare issues exist around *dhabihah* and *shechita*, particularly in the light of current research into recoverable pre-stunning that is, arguably, permissible according to halal rules (Salamano et al, 2013) and is accepted by the HFA and, as has been seen, by equivalent authorities in several predominantly Muslim countries. Furthermore, the requirements of *shechita* are not self-evidently incompatible with post-cut stunning, with an animal first having its carotid arteries cut by the neck incision and then being quickly stunned to ensure, as soon as possible after the cut, that it is unconscious. In Britain, there is debate and divergence within religious communities about slaughter methods and, among Muslims, a widespread acceptance of recoverable stunning as compatible with *dhabihah* slaughter and halal consumption.

Nevertheless, in the moral panic of February 2014 around 'religious slaughter', animal welfare was primarily the presenting issue for irrational, unarticulated anxieties about the place of Muslims in British society. The purportedly moral discourse evinced little serious engagement with either religious beliefs or welfare science and contributed to what, over the past decade, has been a documentable hardening of attitudes on the part of people who identify themselves with either the religious or welfare 'sides' of the debate. The HMCUK (2014) presents non-stun slaughter as a requirement of *dhabihah*, even though the practice of this slaughter method far predates modern stunning technology. Animal-welfare experts rightly cite scientific evidence that, without some form of stunning, *dhabihah* or *shechita* slaughter undermine welfare (Farm Animal Welfare Council 2009b, p 207; 2003, p 201).

Moral panic is a poor substitute for serious moral debate or argument based on knowledge and reflection. It is a foil for unacknowledged anxieties and insecurities and a means by which people who themselves engage in morally ambiguous practices (most obviously in this case, the eating of meat) avoid self-interrogation or public accountability. In the absence of proper moral debate, outcomes are determined in the political realm, in which they are usually the product of expedience and compromise. European Union regulations affirm the importance of states' continuing to allow derogation from stunning on the grounds of respect for 'freedom of religion and the right to manifest religion or belief in worship, teaching, practice and observance' under article 10 of the human rights charter (Anon, 2009). In a civilised, tolerant society, such freedoms are important. Nevertheless, to justify particular practices on such general 'religious' grounds as these has the effect of excluding the possibility of discussion about them. As has been shown, there is no homogeneous group of 'religious' people in Britain advocating slaughter by a particular method. Rather, views are diverse and there is disagreement over the specifics of what should be permitted and what prohibited. Among Muslims, differing interpretations of key Qur'anic passages figure prominently in the scholarly debate (Siddiqui, 2012). In general, Sunni teaching has allowed Muslims to consume the meat of members of other religious groups, including Christians, whereas Shi'ite teaching has prohibited this. Significantly, most British Muslims have family origins in Pakistan, Bangladesh or India, where the Sunni sect predominates.

Furthermore, religious considerations do not necessarily compete with those of animal welfare. On the contrary, animals raised and slaughtered in a religious context that conforms with the halal or kosher requirements should have lived a good life.[5] This includes a good death, in which the experience of pain is minimised. The HFA definition of halal stipulates that, when presented for slaughter, an animal must be in good health and be slaughtered by a Muslim reciting the *tasmiya* (see also Masri, 2007, pp 145–53) or *shahada*.[6] This effectively outlaws mechanical slaughter methods,[7] requiring each animal to be treated as an individual. Shechita UK (2009) indicates that an animal to be slaughtered must not have been caused pain, must have been well fed and be unmutilated. In cases where stunning is resisted, this is likely to be impelled by requirements such as these that, in historical perspective, have promoted farm animal welfare by prohibiting disfigurement or other harmful acts prior to slaughter. This indicates commendable moral and legal motives underlying Islamic and Jewish approaches to animal slaughter that were unrecognised in the 'religious slaughter' debate. The real debate to be opened concerns how these should inform practice in the present day.

Notes

[1] These are minimum numbers because the FSA figures relate to a sample week, during which not all premises licensed to perform *dhabihah* necessarily did so.

[2] Percussive stunning is accepted by some Muslim authorities in Germany and Africa.

[3] For bovines, some form of pre-stunning brings benefits for slaughter-line management through quickly immobilising a large and potentially dangerous animal. Reversible electrical stunning is little used, despite the considerable potential of the single-pulse ultra-high current (SPUC) system (Robins et al, 2014).

[4] It is extremely likely that meat from *shechita* slaughter enters the non-kosher market, because only the front half of a slaughtered animal is deemed to be kosher.

[5] A good life is a key concept in animal welfare (Farm Animal Welfare Council, 2009a, p 16).

[6] The *tasmiya* is: 'In the name of Allah, the most Gracious, the most Merciful'. The *shahada* is: 'There is no god but Allah, Muhammad is the messenger of Allah'.

[7] This point has recently been clarified by the HFA.

References

Anon (2012) 'Polish ritual slaughter illegal, court rules', 28 November, www.bbc.co.uk/news/world-europe-20523809 (accessed 7 August 2014).

Anon (2009) 'Council Regulation (EC) No 1099/2009 of 24 September 2009 on the protection of animals at the time of killing', *Official Journal of the European Union*, 18 November, L 303: 1–30.

Brown, C. (2009) *The death of Christian Britain: Understanding secularisation 1800–2000* (2nd edn), London: Routledge.

Cohen, S. (2002) *Folk devils and moral panic*, London: Routledge.

Coveney, J. (2006) *Food, morals and meaning: The pleasure and anxiety of eating* (2nd edn), London: Routledge.

Farm Animal Welfare Council (2003) *Report on the Welfare of Farmed Animals at Slaughter or Killing. Part 1: Red Meat Animals*, London: DEFRA.

Farm Animal Welfare Council (2009a) *Farm Animal Welfare in Great Britain: Past, Present and Future*, London: DEFRA.

Farm Animal Welfare Council (2009b) *Report on the Welfare of Farmed Animals at Slaughter or Killing. Part 2: White Meat Animals*, London: DEFRA.

Farouk, M.M. (2013) 'Advances in the industrial production of halal and kosher meat', *Meat Science*, vol 95, pp 805–20.

Ferrari, S. and Bottoni, R. (2010) 'Legislation regarding religious slaughter in the EU member, candidate and associated countries', www.dialrel.eu/images/report-legislation.pdf.

Food Standards Agency (2012) 'Results of the 2011 FSA Animal Welfare Survey in Great Britain', http://multimedia.food.gov.uk/multimedia/pdfs/board/fsa120508.pdf.

HFA (Halal Food Authority) (2014) 'Definition of halal', http://halalfoodauthority.com/resources/definition-of-halal (accessed 7 August 2014).

HMCUK (Halal Monitoring Committee UK) (2014) 'Issues of mechanical slaughter and stunning', at www.halalhmc.org/IssueOfMSandStunning.htm (accessed 7 August 2014).

Masri, A.-H.B.A. (2007) *Animal welfare in Islam*, Markfield: Islamic Foundation.

Maurer, D. and Sobal, D. (1995) *Eating agendas: Food and nutrition as social problems,* New York: de Gruyter.

Noble, G. (2012) 'Where's the moral in moral panic? Islam, evil and moral turbulence', in G. Morgan and S. Poynting (eds) *Global Islamophobia: Muslims and moral panic in the west*, Farnham: Ashgate, pp 215–31.

Robins, A. et al (2014) 'The efficacy of pulsed ultrahigh current for the stunning of cattle prior to slaughter', *Meat Science*, vol 96, pp 1201–9.

Salamano, G. et al (2013) 'Acceptability of electrical stunning and post-cut stunning among Muslim communities: A possible dialogue', *Society and Animals*, vol 21, pp 443–58.

Sapontzis, S. (ed) (2004) *Food for thought: The debate over eating meat*, Amherst, NY: Prometheus.

Shechita UK (2009) *A guide to Shechita*, www.shechitauk.org/fileadmin/user_upload/pdf/A_Guide_to_Shechita_2009_.pdf (accessed 7 August 2014).

Siddiqui, M. (2012) 'Pig, purity, and permission in Mālikī slaughter', in *The good Muslim: Reflections on classic Islamic law and theology*, New York: Cambridge University Press, pp 67–89.

Spencer, C. (1993) *The heretic's feast: A history of vegetarianism*, London: Fourth Estate.

Thompson, K. (1998) *Moral panics*, London: Routledge.

Wotton, S.B., Zhang, X., McKinstry, J., Velarde, A. and Knowles, T. (2014) 'The effect of the required current/frequency combinations (EC 1099/2099) on the incidence of cardiac arrest in broilers stunned and slaughtered for the Halal market', *PeerJ PrePrints*, https://peerj.com/preprints/255v1.pdf (accessed 17 March 2015).

THREE

From genuine to sham marriage: moral panic and the 'authenticity' of relationships

Michaela Benson and Katharine Charsley

Introduction

In this chapter, we deconstruct the moral panic around 'sham marriage' – otherwise known as marriages of convenience or marriage for immigration advantage – in Britain. We trace the moral panic over sham marriage, through its visual and provocative depiction in media coverage (newspaper articles, investigatory documentaries) to its propagation and perpetuation in the UK government's continuing project of managing immigration. Marriage-related migration and settlement are a significant challenge to efforts to cap immigration, resulting in attempts to redraw the moral boundaries of immigration policy. Media and policy representations of 'sham marriage' must therefore be understood in this context in terms of the strategic positioning of moral entrepreneurs.

The chapter first outlines how immigration policy relating to spousal migration has come to include reference to 'sham marriage', the identification of such marriages becoming a mechanism for controlling immigration. We highlight how these policies sit within a wider context that promotes immigration as a challenge to moral order, revealing how current political discourse about 'sham marriage' demonstrates many of the characteristics of moral panic. Through a review of Home Office documents, we demonstrate how 'sham marriage' has become firmly embedded in government policy and discourse about marriage-related migration.

Immigration policy, spousal migration and 'sham marriage'

The current management of spousal migration in the UK has a long history, recounted elsewhere (Wray, 2011; Charsley and Benson, 2012). This system contains provision for spousal settlement, although it is clear that successive governments have sought ways of limiting the inflow of spouses. Such provision is underwritten by the UK's adherence to Article 8 of the European Convention on Human Rights on the right to family life. Given that the definition of 'sham marriage' almost certainly precludes the possibility of a family life that would otherwise be protected by Article 8, identifying and excluding such marriages has become a crucial part of the UK government's efforts to manage migration.

The Home Office 'considers sham marriage to be one of the most significant threats to immigration control' but 'acknowledges that its intelligence on the problem is incomplete' (Vine, 2013, p 3). The principal source of data on sham marriage used by the UK government is reports of suspicions about marriage officiates. Since 1999, the duty to report suspicious marriages (by registrars) has been enshrined in the Immigration and Asylum Act 1999, section 24. This reads:

> (5) 'Sham marriage' means a marriage (whether or not void) –
>
> (a) entered into between a person ('A') who is neither a British citizen nor a national of an EEA State other than the United Kingdom and another person (whether or not such a citizen or such a national); and
>
> (b) entered into by A for the purpose of avoiding the effect of one or more provisions of United Kingdom immigration law or the immigration rules.

In addition, the reason given in the 2002 immigration White Paper for proposing to extend the probationary period before spousal settlement from one to two years was to test the genuineness of marriage (Home Office, 2002, p 100).

Wray highlights that since 2005 there has been a renewed government focus on marriages of convenience, accompanied by significant new legislation, leading her to conclude that we have entered a new phase characterised by 'the hunting of sham marriage' (Wray, 2006, p 313). In February of that year, the Certificate of Approval (CoA) scheme was introduced, requiring that non-EEA nationals subject to immigration control (except those with Indefinite Leave to Remain) must seek permission from the Home Office to marry, irrespective of the status of their partner. The adoption of this mechanism was claimed to be a way of prohibiting sham marriage.

Irregular migrants or those with insufficient time left on their visa were refused approval to marry under this scheme, while asylum seekers had to wait for the outcome of their asylum case before receiving a decision on their application. This had a fee of £135 (later increased to £295). In 2006 the scheme was judged by the High Court as disproportionate and discriminatory against those lawfully present, a finding upheld for all migrants on appeal to the Court of Appeal and, finally, the House of Lords.[1] The fixed fee was also judged as an unlawful interference with the right to marry as laid out in the European Convention on Human Rights. Rather than assessing the genuineness or not of the proposed marriage, it had been used as a blanket prohibition on all those who did not have the right immigration status. Partially suspended in 2006, in 2009 the fixed fee was removed, and in 2011 the scheme was finally brought to a close.

In July 2011, the Home Office published a consultation paper in which the government set out a series of proposals for changes to the regulation of family migration (Home Office, 2011). While other forms of family migration were considered in the consultation, its primary focus was on the migration and settlement of spouses and partners. This consultation paper marked a shift in the presentation of key problems in the regulation of such migration, in that sham marriage was discussed before and at greater length than forced marriage, which had had a higher profile in previous discussion (see, for example, Home Office, 2002, 2007). This consultation resulted in the inclusion of new measures aimed specifically at preventing immigration advantage through sham marriage or civil partnership in the 2013 Immigration Bill. The proposed referral and investigation scheme would 'provide the Home Office with more time, information and evidence before the marriage or civil partnership takes place as a basis for identifying, and taking effective enforcement or other immigration action against sham cases' (Home Office, 2013, p 4). If fully introduced in 2015, the mechanics of this process for foreign nationals wishing to marry in England and Wales include increasing the documentation required; an extended notice period (which can be further extended in the case of suspicions); having their applications for marriage assessed by the Home Office against intelligence and evidence-based risk profiles; and the possibility of enforcement action against both parties – for example, removal, curtailment of leave, prosecution for criminal offence (Home Office, 2013). Such measures are further framed around goals of deterrence, improved risk assessment, improved operational response and tackling wider criminality and abuse.

Although not included in the resulting changes to the Immigration Bill, the earlier consultation on family migration had included as its aim finding an 'objective way of identifying whether a relationship is genuine and continuing or not' (Home Office, 2011, p 16). It proposed 'to define more clearly what constitutes a genuine and continuing relationship, marriage or partnership' by setting out 'factors or criteria for assessing whether a relationship, marriage or partnership is genuine and continuing' (Home Office, 2011, p 16). In addition to the plain judgement of whether the union was entered into solely for immigration purposes, these factors included:

- the ability of the couple to provide accurate details about each other and their relationship (with account taken of arranged marriages)
- the ability to communicate in a mutually understood language
- plans for the practicalities of living together in the UK as a couple
- having been in a relationship for at least 12 months prior to the visa or leave to remain application
- the relative ages of the couple

- the nature of the wedding ceremony or reception (for example, few or no guests, the absence of significant family members or the presence of 'complete strangers')
- previous spousal migration or sponsorship of spousal immigration
- a 'compliant history of visiting or living in the UK'.

What becomes clear, as Wray (2006) has also shown, is that marriages that appear to differ from the norm are regarded with suspicion: concerns over sham marriage remain at the forefront of the government's efforts to manage marriage-related migration and have real effects. Furthermore, such controls assume an easily identifiable 'real' marriage.

Moral panic and immigration

In the preface to the third and fourth editions of his seminal work *Folk Devils and Moral Panic* (2002, 2011), Cohen outlines how the characteristics of moral panics have changed. While in the original text he highlighted how moral panics came about, founded on the mismatch between generations, he now stresses that, particularly in the post-9/11 world, immigration is the source of considerable moral panic:

> Governments and media start with a broad public consensus that first, we must keep out as many refugee-type foreigners as possible; second, these people always lie to get themselves accepted; third, that strict criteria of eligibility and therefore tests of credibility must be used. For two decades, the media and the political elites of all parties have focused attention on the notion of 'genuineness' ... 'bogus' refugees and asylum seekers have not really been driven from their home countries because of persecution, but are merely 'economic' migrants, attracted to the 'Honey Pot' of 'Soft Touch Britain'. (Cohen, 2011, p xxii)

The process that Cohen (2011) outlines bears a startling resemblance to how the Coalition government has approached immigration more generally, not only covering economic migrants and refugees but more recently even extending into the discussion of intra-EU migrants. In the case of immigration, moral panic is founded on the immigrant threat to the moral order. Beyond this, however, it becomes clear that such panics may have and have had a real bearing on how the 'problem' of immigration is subsequently addressed. This is fundamentally about border control, and the construction of the undesirable other. As Dauvergne argues:

> Capturing the moral panic about extralegal migrants and enshrining it in law allows governments control that their borders lack. When a part of the population is labeled 'illegal' it is excluded from within (Dauvergne, 2008, p 18).

Moral panics about immigration thus feed into and influence government discourse and policies. Recognising the moral panic that may lie at the core of these provides important context for understanding the resulting legal and policy responses to immigration (Dauvergne, 2008). It seems likely, as the case of sex trafficking outlined below reveals, that moral panics about immigration are here to stay and that they have very real consequences for governance and regulation within the UK. Indeed, what is particularly notable about the moral panic regarding immigration is that the moral entrepreneurs, those individuals and groups in society who bring the moral panic to the attention of the general public, are precisely the government and the media (Finney and Simpson, 2009).

A significant body of literature relating to immigration and moral panic concerns sex trafficking (see, for example, Weitzer 2005, 2007; Dauvergne 2008; Cree et al, 2014). The discourse on trafficking focuses on the ills of the global sex trade, and is founded on a moral order that condemns the sex industry. As Dauvergne (2008) argues, the focus on the 'victims' – those trafficked – shields the power dynamics that maintain the status quo, and thus results in the continuance of trafficking (see also Weitzer, 2005, 2007). This discourse about trafficking, in its over-simplication of the social problem, does not provide real-world solutions for those dealing with trafficked people, for example, social workers (Cree et al, 2014).

The literature on moral panic often presents a causal relationship, whereby moral panic is identified and thus mechanisms are put into place to control the alleged social problem at the root of this. There is, however, another way of considering moral panic, presenting it instead as a smokescreen. This is clear in the work of Hall et al (1978), which shows how mugging became a moral panic that conveniently detracted attention from the crisis affecting the working classes. In this respect, he shows that the government and media involvement in promoting moral panic may be intentional, masking and shielding wider social change and problems. This sense of intentionality, and the links to the wider social context, are important in considering the current moral panics about immigration; indeed, as Rohloff and Wright (2010) argue, it is this latter context, and the production of moral panic, that is often missing from the research on moral panics.

'Sham marriage' and the moral order

Concern over marriages of convenience, 'sham' or bogus marriage marks contemporary British immigration debates, with the terminology being adopted in official documentation and media reports. In the context of wider moral panics about immigration, the current moral panic about 'sham marriages' can be seen as distinct. This is because it is a moral panic drawn along two axes, with the moral order being threatened both by immigration and by the perceived misuse of marriage. With increasing unmarried cohabitation, single parenthood and divorce, marriage may have lost its dominant position as the only socially correct route to coupledom and parenthood, but marriage remains a hegemonic ideal (Gross, 2005). Non-migrants may legally enter into a marriage for any reason, but the ideal of marriage based on intimacy and romantic love is reflected in stereotypes of those (particularly women, as in the figure of the 'gold-digger') perceived to marry for social or economic gain. Such cases are, however, generally merely the subject of ridicule in comparison to the moral outrage and legal measures reserved for cases where immigration benefits accruing to a spouse are suspected as motivating a marriage:

> I wasn't convinced that there was a lot of romance knocking around. They certainly did not know much about each other and were uncomfortable talking about it. And the guests, they looked like they'd been whipped up to come in the last couple of days … everything that I saw and everything I felt when I was with them felt like two strangers walking into a room and then coming out as man and wife. (Richard Bilton in BBC, 2011)

> Today I can reveal new plans to crack down on people who seek to abuse our marriage laws to stay here illegally. Hundreds of sham marriage operators have been caught since this Government came to power – including a vicar jailed for staging 300 faked ceremonies. Now I want to stop these sham ceremonies happening in the first place by changing marriage laws to allow for services to be delayed for investigations. (May, 2012)

There is additional suspicion of organised criminal activity surrounding sham marriages, and there have been several arrests in the UK of alleged 'fake marriage gangs'.

It is clear that sham marriage has become a moral panic; the media depiction and government mobilisation exhibit all the characteristics outlined in Cohen's (2002, 2011) insightful framing of immigration as moral panic. The current discourse of the need to drive down the numbers of immigrants in the country, and to get immigration under control, is repeatedly stated. Immigrants are presented not only as taking British jobs, but also as claiming benefits and thus depriving needy British subjects. Marriage-related migration is one of the few remaining entry routes into the country, and so it is, at least in the minds of government and some media outlets, also ripe for abuse. 'Sham marriage' is presented as the ultimate deception, whereby those desperate to gain entry to the country misuse marriage as a way of ensuring immigration. The solution that the government has implemented is to introduce systems of social control aimed at reducing the instances of such abuse of the immigration system and protecting marriage as an institution. This moral panic clearly rests upon a binary distinction between genuine and fake marriages. Such binaries are largely mythical, presuming that there are clear criteria by which genuine marriages may be assessed. Similarly, it becomes clear that these judgements rely additionally on normative understandings of how marriage is constituted.

Unlike other moral panics regarding immigration, such as trafficking, for the most part there is no underlying ambivalence to the panic, as the migrants themselves are presented not as victims but as a threatening Other. The result of this is that the panic itself is not easily destabilised or defused and has become a more stable and unquestioned basis on which to build regulation, monitoring and control of immigrant populations. The panic has bred 'real effects' through policies, governance and regulation aimed at countering the instance of sham marriage.

Conclusion

The recognition that the discourse about sham marriage has been mobilised by the government as a moral panic raises further questions about the underlying motivations behind this. Sham marriage has without doubt been constructed as a significant social problem, despite any systematic evidence of the numbers of such marriages taking place. Through generating fear and loathing of the would-be abusers of the British marriage and immigration systems, the government has sought to introduce legislation that, while appearing to deal with a social problem, has introduced further measures to control immigration. At this point in time it is also particularly convenient to present immigrants as undeniably problematic for society. In this way, the government and the media detract attention from other public concerns, namely the impact of the government cuts to welfare and pending changes in the job market, in a way not dissimilar to that outlined by Hall et al (1978) in the case of mugging. That these migrant 'others' are presented as offending the British public's sensibilities regarding marriage, in addition to the alleged threat that they present to British jobs and welfare, has the useful potential to sway public opinion and generate support for anti-immigration logics.

Note

[1] *R (on the application of Baiai and others) v SSHD* [2006] EWHC 823 (Admin); *R (on the application of Baiai) v SSHD* [2006] EWHC 1035 (Admin); *R (on the application of Baiai) v SSHD* [2006] EWHC 1454 (Admin); *SSHD v Baiai and others* [2007] EWCA Civ 478; *R (on the application of Baiai and others) v SSHD* [2008] UKHL 53.

References

BBC (2011) 'My big fat fake marriage', *Panorama* (24 March).

Charsley, C. and Benson, M. (2012) 'Marriages of convenience and inconvenient marriages: regulating spousal migration to Britain', *Journal of Immigration, Asylum and Nationality Law*, vol 26, no 1, pp 10–26.

Cohen, S. (2002) *Folk devils and moral panic*, London: Routledge.

Cohen, S. (2011) *Folk devils and moral panic*, London: Routledge.

Cree, V.E., Clapton, G. and Smith, M. (2014) 'The presentation of child trafficking in the UK: an old and new moral panic', *The British Journal of Social Work*, vol 44, no 2, pp 418–33.

Dauvergne, C. (2008) *Making people illegal: What globalization means for migration and law*, Cambridge: Cambridge University Press.

Finney, N. and Simpson, L. (2009) *'Sleepwalking to segregation'? Challenging myths about race and migration*, Bristol: Policy Press.

Gross, N. (2005) 'The detraditionalization of intimacy reconsidered',. *Sociological Theory*, vol 23, no 3, pp 286–311.

Hall, S., Critcher, C., Jefferson, T., Clarke, J. and Roberts, B. (1978) *Policing the crisis: mugging, the state and law and order*, Basingstoke: Macmillan.

Home Office (2002) *Secure Borders, Safe Haven: Integration with Diversity in Modern Britain*, UK: The Stationery Office.

Home Office (2007) *Marriage to Partners from Overseas: a consultation paper*, London: Home Office.

Home Office (2011) *Family migration: a consultation*, London: The Stationery Office.

Home Office (2013) *Sham marriages and civil partnerships: background information and proposed referral and investigation scheme*, London: The Stationery office.

May, T. (2012) 'Sham Busters', *The Sun*, (26 August) www.thesun.co.uk/sol/homepage/news/politics/4505102/Theresa-May-Lets-close-door-on-illegal-immigrants-and-fake-marriages.html (accessed 17 March 2013).

Rohloff, A. and Wright, S. (2010) 'Moral panic and social theory beyond the heuristic', *Current Sociology*, vol 58, no 3, pp 403–19.

Vine, J. (2013) *A Short Notice Inspection of a Sham Marriage Enforcement Operation* (Independent Chief Inspector of Borders and Immigration) London: The Stationery Office.

Weitzer, R. (2005) 'The growing moral panic over prostitution and sex trafficking', *The Criminologist*, vol 30, no 5, pp 1–4.

Weitzer, R. (2007) 'The social construction of sex trafficking: ideology and institutionalization of a moral crusade', *Politics and Society*, vol 35, no 3, pp 447–75.

Wray, H. (2006) 'An ideal husband? Marriages of convenience, moral gate-keeping and immigration to the UK', *European Journal of Migration and Law*, vol 8, pp 303–20.

Wray, H. (2011) *Regulating marriage migration into the UK: A stranger in the home*, Farnham: Ashgate.

FOUR

Integration, exclusion and the moral 'othering' of Roma migrant communities in Britain

Colin Clark

Introduction

> What we can see is the moral panic spinning out of control around child abduction in Roma communities … It is demonising not only the Roma in Greece, but will affect the communities here, including Gypsies. It is playing into the view of Gypsies and Roma as child stealers … You can have one suspected case that leads to the headlines that we have seen. People are speculating about massive abduction rings for begging. (Katharine Quarmby interviewed on Channel 4 News, 22 October 2013)

What happens when two different, but related, moral panics collide? When prejudice and hysteria join forces? What impact does racial profiling have on those communities who find themselves in the crosshairs of the state? In late 2013, various central and Eastern European Roma ('Gypsy') communities living in Britain faced an unwelcome and overtly hostile media spotlight. Politicians openly spoke about needing to 'change' the 'behaviour and culture' of Roma migrants who were allegedly behaving in 'intimidating' and 'offensive' ways. Such views were espoused not by marginalised and disgruntled Tory backbenchers but a former Labour Home Secretary (David Blunkett, MP) and the current (at the time of writing) Deputy Prime Minister (Nick Clegg, MP). This moral panic largely centred around themes of integration, asociality and behaviour but also overlapped and merged with existing media and political attention on allegations of Roma being involved in child abduction – initially the case of 'Maria' in Greece and two later cases in Ireland. Roma 'behaviour and culture', viewed in highly static, essentialist, almost colonial terms, *could only do right in doing wrong* and was presented as being in direct contrast to equally static and unproblematically reified 'British values'. At the local level, accusations of 'antisocial' behaviour were direct and forceful: mainly around 'loitering' on street corners, rubbish disposal, noise, criminal activity and sanitation issues. Tabloid and broadsheet media features appeared targeting mainly Slovak and Romanian Roma communities living in Sheffield, Glasgow and Manchester. Roma people, as an undifferentiated whole, were castigated as the nightmarish, 'backward', antisocial 'neighbours from hell' that no one wanted to live beside. Although this particular moral panic was fortunately brief, it arose out of a well-established anti-Roma history and tradition and has left its mark on present and most likely future community relations. This chapter considers these issues, examining the context, terrain and consequences of the moral panic under discussion. This commentary is situated in a body of sociological and anthropological theory that helps to explain how, where and why this moral panic emerged in the way it did. To complement the theory, data from an on-going research project in Glasgow, conducted by the author, is incorporated to illustrate the impacts of moral panics for those communities directly affected (Clark, 2014).

'Roma behaviour' = moral panic

Roma mobility and settlement across Europe has been on-going for several centuries, subject to the same kind of 'push' and 'pull' factors that many migrant groups have had to endure (Matras, 2014a). Similarly, anti-Roma discrimination, violence and deportations across Central and Eastern and Western Europe have ebbed and flowed over the years, dependent on factors that have been mostly external to Roma communities themselves (Pusca, 2012; Stewart, 2012). Recent global austerity crises have given rise to widespread anti-migrant sentiments generally, but Roma have been subject to quite specific forms of targeting across all corners of Europe, especially Hungary, the Czech and Slovak Republics, France and Italy. The fact that such anti-Roma measures and actions are taking place during the 'Decade of Roma Inclusion' (2005–15) is not without bitter irony. Indeed, as National Roma Strategies are being transformed into Local Action Plans it remains to be seen what material impact these plans will have on people's day-to-day lives (Poole, 2010; McGarry, 2012).

The author's on-going research project in Glasgow investigates key themes of welfare, 'integration', empowerment and identity (Clark, 2014). These matters were identified by both researcher and families as being pivotal to their everyday experiences as 'new' migrants in the Govanhill area of the city. Through participant observation and semi-structured interviews, working with Roma families and organisations from the public and voluntary sectors, a picture emerges of a geographic area where challenges and opportunities present themselves in equal measure. It was into this fieldwork domain that the moral panics described above appeared, courtesy of invasive and hostile media attention on the cases of 'Maria' in Greece and the children taken into care in Ireland and subsequent ill-considered statements from senior politicians in England regarding 'problematic' Roma integration and 'behaviour' in UK towns and cities.

Indeed, this small on-going ethnographic research project has taken a micro-sociological and intersectional approach to understanding issues of day-to-day Roma integration and exclusion. Upon reflection, it is the only way such a project could have any chance of success. As Davis (2008, p 68) has argued:

'Intersectionality' refers to the interaction between gender, race, and other categories of difference in individual lives, social practices, institutional arrangements, and cultural ideologies and the outcomes of these interactions in terms of power.

This is a most relevant and pertinent definition, as Davis places *power* at the centre of any discussion surrounding intersectional understandings of 'difference' and interactions across and between different social divisions. The same is true of moral panics, whereby political, economic and social power is crucial in establishing who the 'folk devils' are and who the 'claims makers' or 'moral entrepreneurs' are, to draw on Cohen's (1973) terminology. Another similarity and connection is in the understanding that individual identity and experience, as well as structural and wider cultural matters, are important in accounting for moral panics and discovering where exactly the boundaries lie between structure and agency. Intersectionality can help in untangling this complex scenario, locating the arenas of what King (1988) has termed 'multiple jeopardy'.

The making of a 'Roma' moral panic

C: What are the main challenges with this idea of integration? How is that playing out in Govanhill would you say?

E: Well ... How can we speak of integration when some people don't want to accept you? There needs to be more learning and listening I think ... We can learn from each other and get away from the lazy stereotypes. There is good and bad in all of us, every community. (From Kosice, Slovakia)

Social research cannot be understood without appreciating its social and political context and the external factors that impinge on the research environment. In this regard, in October 2013, Christos Salis, Eleftheria Dimopoulou and 'Maria' were 'actors' on the global media stage and the spotlight burned bright at both home and abroad. A plethora of racialised and reified anti-Roma stereotypes appeared in print and broadcast media and features ran with emotive and conjectured commentaries that tapped into essentialist 'Roma steal children' and 'dark-skinned Roma cannot possibly have white babies' discourses, as well as discussing 'kidnapped' child brides and the general nature of 'untrustworthy', 'anti-social' and 'dangerous' Roma communities (McCaffrey, 2013; Pilditch, 2013; Spencer, 2013).

All too quickly, a full-blown international moral panic was beginning to gather pace regarding Roma and 'child abduction' (Eccles and Martin, 2013; Stack, 2013). From state authorities and public officials, as well as newspaper and TV reporting, the messages being presented to audiences were both clear and consistent regarding Roma. Further, especially in England and France, politicians were lamenting and angst-ridden about Roma communities from Central and Eastern Europe who were settling in their countries and constituencies, attempting to live their lives, seek work and send their children to school. Two interventions stood out in this regard: one from the former Labour Home Secretary, David Blunkett, MP and the other from the current Deputy Prime Minister in the Coalition government, Liberal Democrat Nick Clegg, MP. Respectively, they are quoted as having said:

> We have got to change the behaviour and the culture of the incoming community, the Roma community, because there's going to be an explosion otherwise. We all know that. (David Blunkett, quoted in Engineer, 2013)

> There is a real dilemma ... when they [Roma] behave in a way that people find sometimes intimidating, sometimes offensive. (Nick Clegg, quoted in Bennett, 2013)

How do you change 'behaviour and a culture'? When does 'sometimes' become 'always'? The sentiment, language and expression are telling and worth considering. It is clearly not a discourse of Roma integration and inclusion but, rather, one of their assimilation and exclusion. The diverse and heterogeneous Roma community are spoken of as being one and the same, with no acknowledgement of the differences between, across and within the communities in terms of their language, history and tradition. There are clear charges being laid against 'the Roma' in terms of their behaviour, which is, we are informed, 'intimidating and offensive' and which, if left unchecked, may lead to an 'explosion'. But according to whom? In what way? An assumed majority is spoken of – 'people' – who are drawn upon for the purposes of political rhetoric only. Let's consider a local example to try to establish some facts – always worthwhile when examining the wobbly foundations of moral panics.

A recent 'mapping report' indicated that the majority of Roma families in Scotland stay in Glasgow (some 4,000–5,000 people), with smaller communities in cities and towns such as Edinburgh, Fife and Aberdeen (Social Marketing Gateway, 2013, p 14). Within Glasgow, most Roma families are located in the south-east of the city, in Govanhill. There is a long history of migration and settlement in this ethnically diverse area, where more than 50 languages are spoken daily. Although it was initially Roma from Slovakia and the Czech Republic who moved to the area, dating back to 2004–05, there are now many other communities in Govanhill, such as Romanian and Bulgarian Roma who arrived after accession in 2007–08 (Clark, 2014; Ross, 2013).

At the local level, national anti-Roma statements from 'moral entrepreneurs' such as politicians and newspaper commentators are felt hard and have an impact. As in Manchester, Roma mothers in Govanhill reported that they were constantly anxious and scared of their children being taken into care by the police or social workers, if their children's eye and hair colour failed to match their own or deviated from the crude assumptions of racial profiling (Matras, 2014b). On the streets in Govanhill, conversations about Roma are many and varied, although, as ever, it is the negative comments that are heard loudest. Although far from representative, some of those conversations have featured such pronouncements as:

> "Who are these people? They are the new Irish, son …"
>   "They are probably all criminals."
>   "They are a nightmare for local residents."
>   "Violence and intimidation from the Roma is the norm
> … hanging about in gangs."

"Roma are making Govanhill a bad place to live."
"This place is Ground f***ing Zero ... Govanhell."
"I heard, 15 odd of them ... in a two-bedroom flat!"

The above ethnographic 'soundbites' reflect some of the concerns and anxieties, whether real or imagined, that are expressed by non-Roma residents staying within Govanhill. These comments were heard and gathered in conversations taking place in local parks, supermarkets, shops, taxi-cabs, schools and at various meetings over the last year. The language and terminology appears to follow a familiar pattern, also witnessed in other areas of the UK where Roma have settled, such as Page Hall in Sheffield (Shute, 2013). There are allegations of criminality, public nuisance, sanitation issues, antisocial behaviour, inappropriate rubbish disposal and overcrowding, and a sense that the situation is, as one Govanhill resident who is involved in a local residents' group was quoted as saying, "a big, bubbling pot of tension and something has to be done before it gets too much" (Jade Ansari, quoted in Fletcher, 2013). However, when taken together and looked at objectively, rarely are such claims supported by firm and conclusive evidence from the police and other statutory agencies who work with Roma and other communities in the area (Grill, 2012).

The rhetorical power of such statements far exceeds the truth and bears direct testimony to some of the 'moral panic' arguments proposed by Howard Becker (1963) and Stan Cohen (1973).

This mismatch between fact, truth and evidence will now be reflected on with regard to some of the theoretical issues this topic and research raises.

Discussion

It is prudent to briefly reflect on Stanley Cohen's classic study, *Folk Devils and Moral Panics* (1973) and what it can tell us about this particular situation of the Roma. Cohen argued that a 'panic' occurs when there is an identifiable 'threat', whether real or imagined and whether arising via a group or an episode, to established societal norms, interests and conservative, mainstream values. Such 'panics' occur when a localised or national 'concern' emerges that identifies a group as being detrimental to the 'good' of society. Often this concern is demonstrated and vocalised in overtly hostile and confrontational ways, through illustrating that 'they' are not like 'us' (Thompson, 1998). This is often perpetuated and legitimised at all levels of society: politicians, local councillors, the press and other agencies can act to reinforce, condone and legitimise the vilification of tagged 'folk devils'. Once a consensus is reached whereby the majority of the population agree that members of a certain identifiable group are 'folk devils' who pose a 'threat' to society. then action in the form of draconian policies, legislation, practices, occurs to dampen the supposed 'threat.'

More often than not, the weight and consequences of such actions are gravely disproportionate to the perceived 'threat' (Goode and Ben-Yehuda, 1994). To be sure, the aim is not to tackle any underlying material issues that may have caused the initial situation, such as youth unemployment in Cohen's study, but, rather, to radically reinforce established societal norms. Indeed, although Cohen's example was focused on youth culture and the media (the Mods and the Rockers of the 1960s on the south coast of England), his theoretical framework can usefully analyse the position of Roma communities in Britain. They habitually face extreme scorn and contempt while doing little more than moving to Britain to improve their prospects, engage in a variety of employment practices and raise their children.

Aside from Cohen, we can also turn to the work of anthropologists such as Mary Douglas (1966) and Fredrik Barth (1969) in a constructive manner. Likewise, the work of sociologists such as Howard Becker (1963) and Erving Goffman (1963) stand out as having something to offer the discussion. For example, Douglas and Goffman, in slightly different ways, look at 'spoiled identity' and how the stigmatised are regarded by the 'normals', in Goffman's terms. Douglas's interest in how issues of dirt and waste are thought of (simply put, 'matter out of place') resonates with neighbourhood responses to how sections of particular Roma communities use social/public space in a way that transgresses local residents' conceptions of 'normal' behaviours and actions. In short, Roma socialising is perceived as 'loitering with intent' because it is done outside rather than inside, due to overcrowding in housing provision. Barth's work allows us to understand the relational processes at work in communities and illustrates how inclusion and exclusion are fostered or prevented, based on perceived 'ethnic differences' that are presented as insurmountable challenges, often reduced to 'language difficulties' faced by new migrant communities. For Becker (1963), the rules of the game are laid down by 'moral entrepreneurs' (both creators and enforcers) who stake a claim in the debates and set the terms of engagement, making outlandish claims (often with little evidence) in order to bolster their own fixed (power) positions. Viewed from these conceptual perspectives, it is evident that the views of the claims makers and moral entrepreneurs are contradicted by the voices and experiences of Roma people themselves and their supporters. It's interesting to note that such normative statements about Roma 'behaviour and culture' are heavily classed, gendered and racialised, with historical precedents in terms of how other migrant communities have been greeted in the past as well as setting new benchmarks for the kind of reception future, incoming migrant communities might face (Tyler, 2013).

Conclusion

This chapter has examined a particular occasion of moral panic in relation to Roma communities in Britain in which the interest of politicians and the media in Roma 'behaviour and culture' dovetailed, in late 2013, with a European focus on alleged Roma child-abduction cases. The timing was, perhaps, crucial in driving the moral panic onto the front pages of newspapers; the spotlight had certainly been extended in scope and more brightly illuminated. But it was not just fate or chance that delivered this blow; centuries of anti-Roma prejudice fuelled and sustained the panic once it had emerged. Indeed, the panic contained some of Cohen's key ingredients: (1) an identified, racially profiled 'enemy within' who could, however simplistically, be differentiated from Goffman's 'normals'; (2) alleged transgressions from the assumed 'moral order' that again mark the communities as 'outside' normal community boundaries; and (3) a hostile media and political climate keen to stamp a mark of authority on 'British values' and to impose limits on Roma migration. Moving forwards, how can such moral panics regarding Central and Eastern European Roma communities in Britain be avoided or, better, challenged? Clearly, more effective responses to anti-Roma rhetoric need to be delivered, by Roma activists, academics and journalists themselves. Indeed, more broadly, Roma people and families must be consulted about the projects that are focused on their own communities; Roma need to be 'given voice' (take and claim it?) and resist their own demonisation and racial profiling. This will require building capacity within the Roma community, in the form of Roma mediators, teachers and facilitators, and especially the empowerment of both young and old Roma women. More so, the development of knowledge, skills, pride and public recognition of Roma ethnicity is a crucial factor, including training and cultural awareness-raising activities. All this can be done, of course, with *gadzhe* (non-Roma) supporters, but they must be willing to take a secondary, following role rather than a primary, leading role.

References

Barth, F. (1969) 'Introduction', in F. Barth (ed) *Ethnic groups and boundaries*, Boston: Little Brown & Company.

Becker, H. (1963) *Outsiders: Studies in the sociology of deviance*, New York: The Free Press.

Bennett, O. (2013) 'Thousands call Nick Clegg's LBC radio show to back Daily Express petition on EU migration', *Daily Express* (31 October), www.express.co.uk/news/uk/440366/Thousands-call-Nick-Clegg-s-LBC-radio-show-to-back-Daily-Express-petition-on-EU-migration (accessed 24 July 2014).

Clark, C. (2014) 'Glasgow's Ellis Island? The integration and Stigmatisation of Govanhill's Roma population', *People, Place and Policy*, vol 8, no 1, pp 34–50, http://extra.shu.ac.uk/ppp-online/glasgows-ellis-island-the-integration-and-stigmatisation-of-govanhills-roma-population/ (accessed 27 July 2014).

Cohen, S. (1973) *Folk devils and moral panics*, St Albans: Paladin.

Davis, K. (2008) 'Intersectionality as buzzword: A sociology of science perspective on what makes a feminist theory successful', *Feminist Theory*, vol 9, no 1, pp 67–85.

Douglas, M. (1966) *Purity and danger: An analysis of concepts of pollution and taboo*, London: Routledge and Kegan Paul.

Eccles, L. and Martin, A. (2013) 'Now blonde girl found at Roma home in Ireland: blue-eyed child of seven is led away by Police and social workers', *Daily Mail* (22 October), www.dailymail.co.uk/news/article-2471521/Blonde-girl-Roma-gypsy-home-Ireland.html (accessed 24 July 2014).

Engineer, C. (2013) 'David Blunkett issues riot warning over Roma migrants', *Daily Star* (13 November), www.dailystar.co.uk/news/latest-news/350447/David-Blunkett-issues-riot-warning-over-Roma-migrants (accessed 24 July 2014).

Fletcher, A. (2013) 'Roma migrants: could the UK do more to integrate them?' BBC Radio 4, *The Report* (13 December), www.bbc.co.uk/news/uk-25322827 (accessed 26 July 2014).

Goffman, E. (1963) *Stigma: Notes on the management of spoiled identity*, Englewood Cliffs, NJ: Prentice-Hall.

Goode, E. and Ben-Yehuda, N. (1994) *Moral panics: The social construction of deviance*, Oxford: Wiley-Blackwell.

Grill, J. (2012) '"It's building up to something and it won't be nice when it erupts." Making of Roma migrants in a "multicultural" Scottish neighborhood', *Focaal, Journal of Global and Historical Anthropology*, vol 62, pp 42–54.

King, D.K. (1988) 'Multiple jeopardy, multiple consciousness: The context of a Black feminist ideology', *Signs*, vol 14, no 1, pp 42–72.

Matras, Y. (2014a) 'A Roma reality check', *Guardian* (12 February), www.theguardian.com/commentisfree/2014/feb/12/roma-reality-check (accessed 25 July 2014).

Matras, Y. (2014b) *Roma migrants from Central and Eastern Europe*, policy briefing, University of Manchester (March), www.policy.manchester.ac.uk/media/projects/policymanchester/Policy@Manchester-briefing---Roma-Migrants.pdf (accessed 4 August 2014).

McCaffrey, M. (2013) 'Blonde-haired, blue-eyed girl (7) taken from Roma family in Dublin', *Sunday World* (22 October), www.sundayworld.com/top-stories/news/blonde-haired-blue-eyed-girl-7-taken-from-roma-family-in-dublin (accessed 24 July 2014).

McGarry, A. (2012) 'The dilemma of the European Union's Roma policy', *Critical Social Policy*, vol 32, no 1, pp 126–36.

Pilditch, D. (2013) 'Worldwide hunt for family of girl "stolen by gypsies" in Greece', *Express* (21 October), www.express.co.uk/news/world/438148/Worldwide-hunt-for-family-of-girl-stolen-by-gypsies-in-Greece (accessed 24 July 2014).

Poole, L. (2010) 'National Action Plans for Social Inclusion and A8 migrants: the case of the Roma in Scotland', *Critical Social Policy*, vol 30, no 2, pp 245–66.

Pusca, A. (ed) (2012) *Roma in Europe: Migration, education and representation*, Brussels: International Debate Education Association.

Ross, P. (2013) 'Govanhill: Glasgow's Ellis Island', *Scotland on Sunday* (10 February), www.scotsman.com/lifestyle/govanhill-glasgow-s-ellis-island-1-2783217 (accessed 25 July 2014).

Shute, J. (2013) 'Roma in Sheffield: "when it goes off, it will be like an atom bomb here"', *Telegraph* (16 November), www.telegraph.co.uk/news/uknews/immigration/10452130/Roma-in-Sheffield-When-it-goes-off-it-will-be-like-an-atom-bomb-here.html (accessed 27 July 2014).

Social Marketing Gateway (2013) *Mapping the Roma Community in Scotland: Final Report*, Glasgow: The Social Marketing Gateway, www.socialmarketinggateway.co.uk/news/new-research-mapping-the-roma-community-in-scotland/ (accessed 24 July 2014).

Spencer, B. (2013) 'Maria was "groomed to be a child bride": police claim girl found in gipsy camp was set to be married off at the age of 12 by the couple who adopted her', *Daily Mail* (23 October), www.dailymail.co.uk/news/article-2474417/Maria-groomed-child-bride-Roma-Gypsy-couple.html (accessed 24 July 2014).

Stack, S. (2013) 'Blonde girl taken into care from Roma family in Dublin', *The Herald*, www.heraldscotland.com/news/world-news/blonde-girl-taken-into-care-from-roma-family-in-dublin.22492714 (accessed 25 July 2014).

Stewart, M. (ed) (2012) *The Gypsy 'menace': Populism and the new anti-Gypsy politics*, London; Hurst and Company.

Thompson, K. (1998) *Moral panics*, London: Routledge.

Tyler, I. (2013) *Revolting subjects: Marginalization and resistance in neoliberal Britain*, London: Zed Books.

FIVE

Assisted dying: moral panic or moral issue?

Malcolm Payne

Introduction

This chapter interrogates a phenomenon that, although not a new issue, has captured the public's attention in recent years. The controversy about assisted dying is concerned with whether or in what circumstances it is right for someone to assist another person in committing suicide or otherwise hastening the process of dying. Physician-assisted suicide (PAS) refers to assistance by healthcare professionals. Assisted dying has been a constant in medical ethics. The Hippocratic Oath of the ancient Greeks, for example, required ethical doctors not to 'give a lethal drug to anyone if I am asked, nor will I advise such a plan' (North, 2002). The Oath came to be seen as a general interdiction against assisting patients or others who wished to use medical expertise to die.

After anaesthetics were developed during the 19th century, some doctors advocated using them to relieve pain in the dying phase of life, debates about the ethics of euthanasia raged and there were attempts at legislation (Emanuel, 1994). During the first part of the 20th century, the issue was raised again, in particular by the rise of eugenics and mental hygiene movements, culminating in the rejection of such ideas after the experience of widespread mortality in two world wars, the implementation of eugenic policies by the Nazi regime and the Holocaust.

The illegality and moral unacceptability of assisted dying is therefore clearly the 'established' position in many societies, although this established moral settlement has been challenged by 'right to die' groups and individual campaigners, partly because of public opinion. The British Social Attitudes Survey examined public attitudes to assisted dying, using the same question for 30 years; its most recent report finds that there is widespread and growing public support for assisted dying in some form (Park et al, 2013, p ix). So, assisted dying is clearly a moral issue, but is it a moral panic?

UK legal provision

In most legal jurisdictions, euthanasia and assisted dying are illegal. In the UK, murder and suicide were illegal at common law and murder remains contrary to the Homicide Act 1957. The Suicide Act 1961, section 1, decriminalised suicide, but did not establish a right to commit suicide. Section 2(1) of the Act also created a specific offence, punishable by imprisonment for a term of up to 14 years, of assisting a person to commit suicide (*Nicklinson v A Primary Care Trust*, 2013). By the 'double effect' principle, it is legal for a doctor to prescribe medication or treatment that may hasten death where the purpose is to relieve pain and suffering. It is also lawful to withdraw medical treatment, allowing a condition to take its natural course, even though this is likely to bring about a patient's death. Article 8 of the European Convention on Human Rights, written into UK law by the Human Rights Act 1997, section 1, provides for a right to respect for private and family life (including, by extension, the right to commit suicide, which was withheld in English law). This right is qualified, however, where domestic law provides for exceptions 'in the interests of national security, public safety or the economic well-being of the country, for the prevention of disorder or crime, for the protection of health or morals, or for the protection of the rights and freedoms of others.'

Other legal systems

A number of legal jurisdictions make provision for assisted dying, on varying criteria and using diverse procedures. These include Belgium, the Netherlands, the US state of Oregon (whose legislation dates from

1998, thus making it the first of several US states that now provide for assisted dying) and Switzerland. Such permissive jurisdictions have been used as examples of the successful introduction of assisted dying by campaigners in 'right to die' organisations across the world.

The main arguments

The two main areas of argument are moral and practical. The moral argument in favour of PAS asserts an individual's rights to self-determination and control of their lives. Against PAS, ethical, moral and religious arguments assert the sanctity of life. The practical arguments in favour are that PAS offers relief from suffering, particularly where this becomes unbearable, and the main argument against is the 'slippery slope' argument, which I discuss below.

Seven rights-based arguments for assisted dying are:

- rights to liberty, arguing that freedom is a basic good, permitting individuals to do as they wish, unless they harm others, and prohibition on assisted dying restricts that freedom;
- rights to autonomy and self-determination, arguing that individuals are free to define their own conceptions of good. This individualistic perspective, argued in legal cases in many Western jurisdictions, proposes that life is owned by the person living it, who is free to make quality-of-life decisions;
- rights to privacy, arguing that states, professionals and other individuals should not intervene in important private decisions such as suicide;
- rights to dignity;
- rights to equality, arguing that, since suicide is legal in most jurisdictions, people who, because of disability, cannot secure their own suicide are treated unequally by the law and the state because they are denied a legal choice available to others. Since people have the right to refuse life-sustaining medical treatment, it is illogical that they are not permitted to take their lives, which amounts to the same thing;

- right to freedom of conscience and religion, arguing that states are imposing a moral prohibition deriving from public opinion or religious belief;
- rights to property, arguing that the individual has rights to ownership of their body and life.

These points are often made in rebuttal of religious or moral arguments about the sanctity of life (Lewis, 2007).

Opponents of assisted dying also present rights-based arguments:

- rights to life, arguing that statements of human rights declare the right to life as inalienable and therefore mandatory;
- rights to equality and equal protection, arguing that legalisation may particularly affect already marginalised groups such as physically and learning disabled people and older people, who may be most subject to other pressures in life, and also to mental disturbance arising from those pressures, or might be more likely to be pressured, subtly or otherwise, to take up a right to die. Also, legalisation of assisted suicide is often proposed only for terminally ill people and people with severe physical disability, and this could be seen as prejudicial treatment favouring people who would not then have equal protection with other citizens.
- rights to property, arguing that our bodies are entrusted to us by God, and that legalisation merely substitutes the state for God as the holder of our bodies as property; for example, it may be said that the state has an interest in the preservation of citizens' lives;rights to autonomy, arguing that legalisation poses a threat to autonomy by establishing the social, cultural and political context of people's personal choices, including for example, financial barriers to palliative and community-based care and a culture saturated by media images of trivialised and apparently justified killings (Lewis, 2007: 35–42).

Lewis's (2007) analysis is that competing and irreconcilable differences in rights-based arguments mean no agreed view can be arrived at that could achieve widespread public support for legislation or policy in either direction.

The practical arguments for and against assisted dying connect with the importance given to healthcare in most societies and to the social role of the medical profession. Although we all die, many people do not dwell on this reality while they are living. Avoiding active discussion of death may be healthy because it allows people to continue with their life tasks, without becoming over-anxious about various risks to their lives. Many of the practical arguments about assisted dying refer to the 'slippery slope' arguments.

- There is a gradation of situations and it is hard to decide between situations where people might agree that assisted dying was desirable and situations where it would be harder to get agreement.
- Physicians would have the right, as with abortion, to opt out of performing assisted suicides: physicians who agreed to do so might become a focus of demand and conflict if campaigning groups opposed their work, in the way that has happened around abortion in some countries.
- Professional practice in health and social care relies on trust; the possibility that a professional might later be involved in decisions about assisted dying might inhibit trust.
- Patients and families may experience conflicts and may fear financial losses to their capital if long-term care is required; this may apply pressure on families and patients to agree to assisted suicide.
- People may change their minds.
- Good care will reduce the impact of feared symptoms, but it may be hard to accept this before the symptoms are relieved; people may not understand what will happen at their death.
- The prognosis that death is imminent may be wrong.
- Anxiety and depression affect many people approaching the end of life, but this is often treatable (Reith and Payne, 2009, chapter 8).

Right-to-die campaigns

Responding this range of concerns a number of 'right to die' organisations have developed, all with similar policies. The World Council of Right to Die Organisations (www.worldrtd.net/), founded in 1980, comprises 52 right-to-die organisations from 26 countries; its slogan is 'Ensuring choices for a dignified death' (World Federation of Right to Die Societies, 2013). However, in the UK its members are not those most prominent at present in campaigning; the greatest prominence belongs to the Campaign for Dignity in Dying (www.dignityindying.org.uk/). There have been substantial committees of inquiry in several countries, and attempts at legislation in the UK, all of which have been surrounded by public controversy.

Alternatives to assisted dying

If we accept that the right-to-die campaigns have identified an important issue in the public mind, what alternative ways exist of dealing with this issue? Three main alternatives are often proposed: firstly, acceptance of the reality of death and suffering; secondly, a case is made for the value of pain and symptom management through palliative care or other medical interventions designed to relive suffering; thirdly, the availability of advance care planning, advance decisions and a lasting power of attorney are stressed.

Suffering

Not everyone who is seriously ill or approaching death seeks to hasten that death, indeed one of the important objectives of end-of-life and palliative care is to support feelings of hope among people approaching the end of life (Reith and Payne, 2009). Many professional writers suggest that it is more common for people to seek any and all forms of treatment for their condition. There may also be differences of view about what constitutes suffering. In a study of patients who requested but were not granted euthanasia in the Netherlands in 2005, it was found that patients and physicians agreed that not all patients who requested euthanasia thought their suffering was unbearable, although they had a lasting wish to die. Patients 'put more emphasis on psychosocial suffering, such as dependence, deterioration, and not being able to participate in life anymore, whereas the physicians refer more often to physical suffering' (Pasman et al, 2009).

Approaching death may be frightening, but nursing, social and psychological support can assist people to experience this successfully. In particular, although there is a high incidence of depression and affective disorder among people approaching the end of life, this is often treatable (Robinson and Scott, 2012). Others argue that dying with dignity comes through the endurance of suffering, and that this is ennobling or has redemptive value for the sufferer. Studies of terminally ill people's attitudes suggest that a desire for death has been found, but it is often transient and may be linked to depression (Brown et al, 1986; Emanuel et al, 2000).

One option for the relief of suffering is the practice of continuous deep sedation until death. This provides for patients who are not yet experiencing major organ failure but who are in severe pain or have other distressing symptoms. Variations in who is given sedation and the settings in which this occurs suggest that there are cultural and organisational differences in different countries that lead to different medical practices (Anquinet et al, 2012).

Care not Killing

Care not Killing is an organisation that opposes changes in the law in assisted dying in the UK (www.carenotkilling.org.uk/). Its name reflects its main argument that palliative healthcare services are an acceptable alternative to assisted dying. Most developed countries provide palliative care, which the World Health Organization's (WHO) policy on cancer care proposes should be integral to public healthcare services everywhere (WHO, 2013). Many countries have developed policy favouring palliative and end-of-life care provision, because of public demand.

In the UK, the most important recent initiative is the National End of Life Care Strategy (Department of Health, 2008), which produced supportive guidance and training. One important element of this programme was the Liverpool Care Pathway (LCP), which aimed to tackle poor quality of care for dying people in hospitals by raising awareness in ward staff when patients were approaching death. It encouraged them to discuss this sympathetically with patients and their families, and to ensure their comfort. The LCP itself became controversial and was discontinued; the controversy illustrates many of the conflicts in public debate about assisted dying.

The LCP was based on hospice practice (Ellershaw and Wilkinson, 2010). It provided a practice protocol, and a service for testing improvement in each of the items of the protocol against a baseline registered by a care organisation or hospital when it started to use the Pathway. Many hospitals appointed coordinators to develop the programme, primarily for older people. A press campaign developed against it, claiming that people were placed on it who were not imminently dying, and this was done without adequate discussion with members of the family and carers. An important aspect of the criticism was of the withdrawal of hydration and nutrition and the implementation of 'Do Not Attempt Cardio-Pulmonary Resuscitation' (DNAR) orders. This is common practice in hospices, since there is evidence that many terminal cancer patients do not need nutrition and hydration and that it may be uncomfortable for them (Partridge and Campbell, 2007). There is also evidence that seriously ill patients do not benefit from cardio-pulmonary resuscitation and may suffer injury or distress if it is used (Ebell et al, 1998).

These widespread policies in palliative care seem to some observers to be in conflict with the intensive life support that enables people to survive a medical crisis until they can recover their own capacity to breathe, drink and eat. Some religious and other ethical views see artificial hydration or feeding as an extension of providing the necessities of life, rather than as a medical intervention. People with such views argue that hydration and possibly artificial feeding should always be available (Craig, 2004).

The press campaign on this issue was so intense that the government set up an inquiry into the LCP, which has led to its replacement by another protocol. Among the problems that the inquiry found (Independent Review of the Liverpool Care Pathway, 2013) was uncertainty about defining when the end of life had been reached, poor decision making, instances where there was a lack of consent, poor communication with patients and their families and poor record completion. There was also a lack of robust research evidence supporting the clinical experience that underlay the creation of the protocol.

Alternative healthcare options: advance care planning

Advance care planning has also been strongly promoted by the National End of Life Care Programme. It aims to produce a system of personalised and integrated planning, engaging people throughout their care careers in thinking about how care services should be organised to meet their personal priorities, including planning for end-of-life care (Payne, 2013). Part of this is using advance directives in which patients specify how they wish to be treated if they lose the capacity to make decisions about their care and medical treatment.

Lasting powers of attorney have replaced previous systems of attorney, allowing a patient to authorise an attorney to act for them if they do not possess or lose the mental capacity to act on their own behalf. Two types of power are available: health and welfare; and property and financial affairs. The patient completes and registers a form specifying their attorney and alternatives, and setting out any requirements and limitations they wish to set (Office of the Public Guardian, 2013). Lasting powers of attorney cannot make provision for someone to make decisions about medical treatment on their behalf.

Discussion and conclusion

Debate about assisted dying engages political debate, campaigning organisations and official reactions to campaigns and public concern.

To many people this is an important moral issue, concerned with significant personal values about what it means to live and to die. Is it appropriate, then, to think of it as a 'moral panic'? Some of the elements of moral panic are present: the raging debate, the press campaigns, the criticisms of moral and practical decisions by the state. Moreover, the raging criticism is of the establishment, and the state representing an established pattern of thinking. The failure of the 'establishment' to react to strong public opinion, the defensiveness of the professionals, the inability to shift legal decisions: all of this suggests outsiders attacking a complacent establishment. Moreover, the press has represented this issue in a personalised, individualistic and moralistic way, dramatising the issue with reference to hard cases, and taking one side in a strongly contested debate about human and individual rights.

Against this, it is clear that this is a centuries-old controversy concerning important personal philosophical and religious values: it is a moral issue that is symbolic of people's views about death and life. It appears to be a panic because of the state's involvement in resisting change in the law and because the state seems to be on the other side of the debate in the criticisms of the way in which end-of-life care is managed in health services. Moreover, the simplification of the issue in press coverage of difficult cases denies the wide range of opinion and the professional uncertainties of those engaged with the issue. This seems unlikely to change, as is illustrated by Lewis's (2007) judgement that the rights-based case for legal change is irresolvable, and the broad agreement of healthcare professionals that there are many practical and ethical issues in the way of agreeing to physician-assisted dying. I suggest that this important and difficult moral issue is disguised as a panic because it seems important to the people engaged in campaigning and because the state has become involved, due to its role in legislation and as the major provider of healthcare services.

References

Anquinet, L., Rietjens, J.A.C., Seale, C., Seymour, J., Deliens, L. and van der Heide, A. (2012) 'The practice of continuous deep sedation until death in Flanders (Belgium), the Netherlands, and the UK: A comparative study', *Journal of Pain and Symptom Management*, vol 44, no 1, pp 33–43.

Brown, J.H., Henteleff, P., Barakat, S. and Rowe, C.J. (1986) 'Is it normal for terminally ill patients to desire death?' *American Journal of Psychiatry*, vol 143, pp 208–11.

Craig, G. (ed) (2004) *No water – no life: Hydration in the dying*, Alsager: Fairway Folio.

Department of Health (2008) *End of Life Care Strategy – promoting high quality care for all adults at the end of life*, London: Department of Health.

Ebell, M.H., Becker, L.A., Barry, H.C. and Hagen, M. (1998) 'Survival after in-hospital cardiopulmonary resuscitation: meta-analysis', *Journal of General and Internal Medicine*, vol 13, pp 805–16.

Ellershaw, J. and Wilkinson, S. (eds) (2010) *Care of the dying: A pathway to excellence* (2nd edn), Oxford: Oxford University Press.

Emanuel, E.J. (1994) 'The history of euthanasia debates in the United States and Britain', *Annals of Internal Medicine*, vol 121, no 10, pp 793–802.

Emanuel, E.J., Fairclough, D.L. and Emanuel, L.L. (2000) 'Attitudes and desires related to euthanasia and physician-assisted suicide among terminally-ill patients and their caregivers', *Journal of the American Medical Association*, vol 284, pp 2460–8.

Independent Review of the Liverpool Care Pathway (2013) *More care, less pathway: a review of the Liverpool Care Pathway*, London: Department of Health.

Lewis, P. (2007) *Assisted dying and legal change*, Oxford: Oxford University Press.

Nicklinson, R (on the application of) v A Primary Care Trust [2013] EWCA Civ 961 (31 July 2013), www.bailii.org/ew/cases/EWCA/Civ/2013/961.html (accessed 11 November 2013).

North, M. (trans) (2002) 'The Hippocratic Oath', in 'Greek medicine', National Library of Medicine, National Institutes of Medicine, www. nlm.nih.gov/hmd/greek/greek_oath.html (accessed 18 November 2013).

Office of the Public Guardian (2013) www.justice.gov.uk/about/opg (accessed 18 November 2013).

Park, A., Bryson, C., Clery, E., Curtice, J. and Phillips, M. (eds) (2013) *British Social Attitudes: The 30th Report*, London: NatCen Social Research.

Partridge, R. and Campbell, C. (2007) *Artificial nutrition and hydration: Guidance for End of Life Care for Adults*, London: National Council for Palliative Care/Association of Palliative Medicine.

Pasman, H.R.W., Rurup, M.L., Willems, D.L. and Onwuteaka-Philipsen, B.D. (2009) 'Concept of unbearable suffering in context of ungranted requests for euthanasia: qualitative interviews with patients and physicians', *British Medical Journal*, vol 339, p b4362.

Payne, M. (2013) 'Extending advance care planning over the care career', *European Journal of Palliative Care*, vol 20, no 1, pp 34–7.

Reith, M. and Payne, M. (2009) *Social work in end-of-life and palliative care,* Bristol: Policy Press.

Robinson, V. and Scott, H. (2012) 'Why assisted suicide must remain illegal in the UK', *Nursing Standard,* vol 26, no 18, pp 40–8.

World Federation of Right to Die Societies (2013) Home page, www. worldrtd.net/ (accessed 21 November 2013).

WHO (World Health Organization) (2013) 'Palliative care is an essential part of cancer control', www.who.int/cancer/palliative/en/ (accessed 21 November 2013).

Afterword:
the moral in moral panics

Heather Lynch

'Panic' is a theme I am familiar with in my work with women who regularly experience extremely distressing situations. It is a natural response to fear, and one that can be managed. Panic of itself is, arguably, morally neutral; how panic is fuelled, steered and exploited is not. Woven through the discussion in this chapter is an interest in moving toward a productive understanding of the function of 'moral panic', in order that it might create stimulus for positive change rather than being steered towards the imperative to cling to problematic norms. This interest underpins the discussion of themes derived from the chapters in this part: the constitution of 'the deviant other' and the discharge of moral responsibility. I then consider the Scottish Government's policy on violence against women, *Equally Safe* (Scottish Government, 2014a), to explore how such themes become operationalised in the context of my practice as a criminal justice social worker in a 'women's' service.

Themes

Each of the chapters in this byte has illuminated a view of the 'undesirable other' as a prerequisite for 'moral panic'. Furedi's Chapter One focused on the contemporary 'other', 'the paedophile'; Benson and Charsley, and Clark, in Chapters Three and Four, respectively, highlighted the 'othering' of those who are perceived as 'not like us' for reasons of cultural difference. These three are, arguably, the most emotive of panics discussed, as they portray clearly recognisible human actors who become readily stereotyped as a homogeneous group. Grumett's discussion of animal welfare in Chapter Two is another emotive topic, as those believed to mistreat animals readily become associated with other immoral practices. In Chapter Five, Payne at the outset acknowledges that the debate on assisted suicide has attracted a more considered discussion, perhaps due to the lack of a 'deviant other' onto whom moral problems can be discharged.

The morality of 'othering' and the devastating effects that this has on individuals, communities and society as a whole have been widely discussed. Post-colonial scholars (Said, 1994; Fanon, 2008) identify significant disadvantages experienced by people who do not conform to the white, western 'norm'. The woeful legacy of colonisers who used the moral imperative to civilise deviant others has endured for centuries and is starkly visible in the contemporary humanitarian crises in Palestine and across Africa. As evidenced in this byte, modern casualties remain as 'folk devils' in the form of dangerous 'immigrants' who have come to disturb our way of life and take our resources. However, the culturally deviant other is not just the preserve of non-western ethnicities.

The majority of people with whom I work experience similar stigma, which might be characterised in Colin Clark's words as 'multiple jeopardy'. The vast majority have grown up in economic poverty and are negated by politicians as 'skivers'. Almost all are in contact with mental health services for substantive mental illness or support with substance misuse; many live in temporary accommodation. Any one of these experiences would readily attract the label of deviant, and together they are a toxic cocktail. Of interest to me is that they are rarely implicated in the most emotive 'moral panics'; perhaps they no longer have the ability to shock. Society does not panic at the deaths of those managing entrenched substance dependency, but the death of an affluent youngster using substances recreationally attracts outrage.

In situations described in this byte moral panics enable the characterisation of not only the deviant other but also the virtuous victim and the rescuer who occupies the moral high ground. Championing the 'virtuous vulnerable' clearly promotes the positive public profile, desired by politicians and institutions seeking public backing. But while the constitution of the deviant other is morally problematic, so too is the production of virtuous vulnerability.

The following section focuses on Equally Safe, a policy that uses the term 'Equally' to draw attention to the political emphasis on equality and, rhetorically at least, egalitarian values. I argue, however, that basing policy on an explicitly moral agenda, not supported by empirical substance, can generate the foundations for 'moral panic' by creating deviant 'otherness' and virtuous vulnerability.

Equally Safe: a case study

Equally Safe lays out the Scottish Government's agenda to 'prevent and eradicate' violence against 'women and girls'. An analysis of this document evidences how policy can serve to reinforce stereotypes while side-stepping and providing a smokescreen in respect of, arguably, more important matters. In no sense do I wish to diminish the harm caused to women who experience such abuse. My purpose in pursing a critical analysis is to show how this approach may in fact contribute to other problems as well as to the issue it seeks to address.

Equally Safe commences by setting out a moral imperative for its existence, drawing on data from the Scottish Crime Survey (Scottish Government, 2014b, 2014c) to argue that violence by men against women and girls is an extremely serious issue requiring focused attention and public resource. The implication in the title is that women and girls are less safe than their male counterparts. The objectives, located in the opening pages, state an aim to create a protective environment within which women and girls can 'thrive as equals' and men will 'desist from all forms of violence against women and girls' (Scottish Government, 2014a, p 21). Statistics quoted state that 80% of domestic violence reported to the police was male toward female and that the root of this problem is 'gender inequality, roles and assumptions' (Scottish Government, 2014a, p 13). Immediately the scene is set where we have a 'deviant other' group in the form of men who act violently toward vulnerable 'women and girls'. While a few short sentences imply that men can also experience violence, the indisputable binary categorisations in this policy narrative are violent men and vulnerable women and girls. The underlying premise of the policy is to create gender equality. However, the reports used to convince that this is a defensible moral focus immediately generate questions on the depiction of men as 'perpetrators', while skimming over equalities issues relevant to all genders.

The *Scottish Crime and Justice Survey 2012/13: Partner Abuse* (Scottish Government, 2014b) states that over the preceding 12 months men were just as likely to experience domestic abuse as were women. Furthermore, men were much less likely to report abuse to the police. This immediately raises questions around the simplistic assertion that women are 'vulnerable victims' and men are 'perpetrators'. Men were also much less likely to report psychological harm as a result of abuse, a point I will return to later. The *Scottish Crime and Justice Survey* (Scottish Government, 2014c) shows that men are more than twice as likely to be victims of violence. Notwithstanding the fact that the assailants are more likely to be men, this shows that it is men who are less safe than women. The landscape created by this statistical report is substantively different to that of Equally Safe. One way of looking at this is that the abuse of men by women is minimal and most likely a response to their abuse and therefore the focus remains on the harm caused to female 'victims'. However, an alternative perspective is that normative gender configurations delimit options for men and anticipate their violence while delimiting expression of emotional distress.

Taking this analysis into account, the moral issue becomes not how best to divide society into 'victims' and 'perpetrators' but how to consider the normative construction of gender in ways that do not stereotype and repress. Butler (1990) provides an analysis of gender as 'performed', not essential or interior. The parameters of performance are delimited by the cultural availability of the social and temporal context. In short, these vary according to the needs and desires of society and therefore are not fixed. Policies that essentialise gender positions obstruct collective responsibility as to how these are produced and, thus, the conditions that make change possible.

Another moral issue that is acknowledged but not developed in Equally Safe is the impact of economic disadvantage. Statistics across crime, partner abuse and mental health evidence this as the single most salient factor in all of these domains. The political motivation to be seen as defending the vulnerable in the face of the 'other' occludes this reality and creates fertile ground for moral panic. Drawing on practice experience, I argue that there are some situations where panic may well be a valid response and that perhaps the issue is not the 'moral panic' in itself but how 'panic' is fuelled and directed.

Implications for practice

The multiple jeopardy of having a criminal history alongside social and economic disadvantage can, for some, make the label 'vulnerable' more attractive than that of 'offender'. As four out of five women offenders are reported to have experienced partner violence, Equally Safe becomes a significant policy lever. It is one of a number of mechanisms that allows women to distance themselves from the deviant negating associations of 'criminal' and instead adopt the more sympathetic position of 'vulnerable' and 'traumatised' victim. The idea that female offenders are emotionally vulnerable is one that is gaining increasing ground in criminal justice scholarship (Gelsthorpe and Hedderman, 2012) and policy (Scottish Government, 2012). There are positives associated with this. Many of the women with whom I work have told chilling tales of horrific violent and sexual abuse from childhood at the hands of both men and women in their lives. Acknowledgement of how this has impacted on their life choices and behaviour offers affirmation. For a few, the medical frames of diagnosis and treatment are useful resources from which they can build a happier, more settled life. However, there are some more insidious issues.

Instilling a sense of vulnerability can become an exchange of one deviancy for another. Individuals may come to view themselves through the medical lens of pathological damage. One woman told me that her (in my view proportionate) excitement at an upcoming event was in fact a manifestation of her personality disorder. Such medicalising has the tendency to individualise, encouraging people to see problems as theirs alone, rather than looking at a more collective societal responsibility. The current policy emphasis in women's criminal justice can further entrench the idea that poor mental health and trauma are 'women's' issues. In fact 'gender' work is read as 'women's' work rather than work that looks at how gender roles and assumptions affect everybody. During group work on domestic abuse I have noticed how some women struggle to identify with the 'victim' identity and recognise the contribution of their own problematic behaviour. Yet, there is a palpable pressure on them to ensure that their experience conforms to the narrative of themselves as victim. Such situations create a complex moral dilemma for me as a practitioner.

I generalise here, because, of course, there are exceptions to the following. However, as most of the people with whom I work have grown accustomed to being cast as dangerous deviants, any opportunity to be positioned outside that frame is generally welcomed, even if this means taking up a different deviant role. In general they will be more condemning of those cast as 'folk devils' than most people would be. From a context where they are conscious of the judgement of others, it appears even more imperative to claim morality. Most have been managing extremely complex situations of multiple disadvantage and are seeking some ways to make sense; therefore frames that reduce and simplify tend to be more attractive than those that broaden the issues and introduce layers of complexity. This creates a dilemma for me. One choice is to work with people in ways that challenge societal norms and the role that they play in reifying disadvantage; however, this risks overwhelming already burdened individuals. Another is to promote the comfort of reinforcing norms by helping women to position themselves as vulnerable victims. It is the difference between getting the best from the status quo or confronting it in order to promote change. The first involves short-term pragmatism, the other a longer-term struggle.

Balancing these tensions is fundamental to my role as a social worker and I am inspired by the work of political philosopher Hannah Arendt (1998). She explores the unique individual ability to act within the world (Veck, 2013). Her focus on the intersection between private interest and public good is highly relevant to criminal justice social work, not simply to assert the need for those convicted of crimes to accept responsibility for the impact of their actions, but to promote a political life that expects active participation in society. She talks of educating 'toward the world'; such an approach lends itself to the moral contemplation called for across the chapters in this part. It is nested in the belief that the political life of the individual constitutes the development of collective values. In doing so it does not seek blame and vulnerability but responsibility and action. In this sense moral panics might have the capacity to generate 'new lines of flight' (Deleuze and Guattari, 1987). The question then becomes not whether moral panics are right or wrong, but what types of change they afford.

Conclusion

I have argued that the moral problem that can arise through reactions to social anxieties is not so much the tendency toward 'moral panic', but how this response is exploited by those who seek to benefit from a position of moral virtue. Analysis of the Scottish Government's policy Equally Safe (2014a) evidences how policy can exploit normative gender roles in order to create a platform for moral leadership. I have argued that the resultant gender stereotyping ignores the devastating ways in which normative gender roles affect men, and in fact contributes to problems for both men and women. Additionally, this focus on gender side-steps the universal issue of the impact of economic disadvantage on all gender orientations.

For me as a social worker, this situation creates a multitude of moral dilemmas that require negotiation with service users, and also with management and colleagues. The crux lies in the reality that adopting mainstream societal norms provides the best opportunity for individual service users, having been cast in deviant roles, to progress toward acceptance. However, this also means not challenging morally questionable stereotypes, either concerning others cast as deviant or about the normative assumptions that contribute to the constitution of conflict.

In conclusion, there is a place for societal panic: the huge gap in opportunity, life expectancy and health between the economically advantaged and disadvantaged is one area worthy of panic; that so many young men find it easier to take their life than to seek help is another. The material in this byte leads me to the view that the societal preference for blame rather than for taking collective responsibility is one of the most pressing moral issues.

References

Arendt, H. (1998) *The human condition*, Chicago: University of Chicago Press.

Butler, J. (1990) *Gender trouble*, Abingdon: Routledge.

Deleuze, G. and Guattari, F. (1987) *A thousand plateaus: Capitalism and schizophrenia*, trans B. Massumi, Minneappolis: University of Minnesota Press.

Fanon, F. (2008) *Black skin, White mask*, London: Pluto Press.

Gelsthorpe, L. and Hedderman, C. (2012) 'Providing for women offenders: the risk of adopting a payment by results approach', *Probation Journal*, vol 59, no 4, pp 374–90.

Said, E. (1994) *Culture and imperialism*, London: Vintage.

Scottish Government (2012) *Commission on Women Offenders*, www.scotland.gov.uk/Resource/0039/00391828.pdf.

Scottish Government (2014a) *Equally Safe: Scotland's strategy or preventing and eradicating violence against women and girls*, www.scotland.gov.uk/Resource/0045/00454152.pdf.

Scottish Government (2014b) *Scottish Crime and Justice Survey 2012/13: Partner Abuse*, www.scotland.gov.uk/Publications/2014/06/5943.

Scottish Government (2014c) *Scottish Crime and Justice Survey 2012/13: Main Findings*, www.gov.scot/Publications/2014/03/9823/downloads.

Veck, W. (2013) 'Participation in education as an invitation to become towards the world: Hannah Arendt on the authority, thoughtfulness and imagination of the educator', *Educational Philosophy and Theory*, vol 45, no 1, pp 36–48.